UNTANGLING
FAITH

UNTANGLING FAITH

Reclaiming Hope in the Questions Jesus Asked

AMBERLY NEESE

Nashville

Amberly Neese is a speaker, humorist, and encourager with a passion for "GRINspiring" others. As a featured speaker for the Aspire Women's Events and the main host/ comedienne for Marriage Date Night, two popular Christian events that tour nationally, she enjoys touching the hearts and minds and funny bones of people all over the country. The Bible says that laughter is good medicine, and she has found it's also like glue—helping the truths of God's Word to "stick." Amberly loves to remind women of the power and hope found in Scripture. Through a flair for storytelling and a love for Jesus, she candidly opens up her story alongside God's Word to encourage others in their walk with Him.

With a master's degree from Biola University, Amberly serves as an adjunct professor at Grand Canyon University and the Master Connector for Inspiring Growth, an organization developed to equip and encourage growth in leaders and businesses. She is the author of *The Belonging Project: Finding Your Tribe and Learning to Thrive*, *Common Ground: Loving Others Despite Our Differences*, and *The Friendship Initiative: 31 Days of Loving and Connecting Like Jesus*. She and her husband, Scott, have two adult children and live in Prescott, Arizona, where they enjoy the great outdoors, the Food Network, and all things *Star Wars*.

Follow Amberly:

 @amberlyneese

 @amberlyneese

 @Amberly Neese - Comedian and Speaker

Website: www.amberlyneese.com

Tour information can also be found at marriagedatenight.com and aspirewomensevents.com.

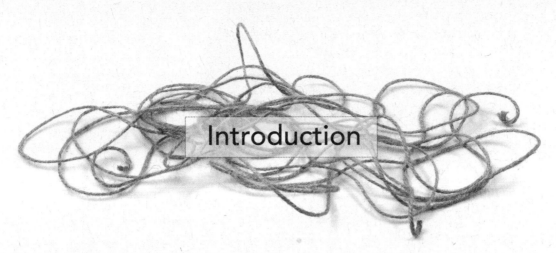

Introduction

One time, I opened my travel jewelry case to find that my necklaces had conspired to intertwine themselves like the freeways in a large city. After hours of struggle and frustration—untwisting, perspiring, unsnarling, using tweezers and needles, and praying—I finally had to cut one of the necklaces to free the ensnared baubles. Although the chains were finally freed from one another's grasp, I was left with a pile of beads, a broken chain, and a nagging sense of failure.

Much like the tangled necklaces in my jewelry case, sometimes it can seem that our faith has become a tangled mess, leaving us unsure of what we believe about God in light of difficult and uncertain circumstances in our lives and our world. When personal pain is compounded by tragedies near and far, cultural conflict, social unrest, and the challenges of an ever-changing world, we can find ourselves tied up in knots by questions that seem to trap us in confusion, discouragement, and disillusionment.

What if I told you that our questions can actually help us untangle our faith and discover a more intimate and satisfying relationship with God? Here's the thing: Jesus loves questions! In the Gospels, Jesus asks over three hundred questions—and He directly answers only three. Does this prove that Jesus wants to be elusive? Absolutely not! By asking so many questions, Jesus invites us to ask, seek, and grapple with our own questions. He wants us to truly know Him in authentic relationship, and a good way to do that is to explore our questions with Him through the lens of the questions He asked while on earth. The Word of God holds the keys to understanding the nature of God more fully, living life more abundantly, and finding joy more readily as we enter into relationship with the Living Word Himself.

Sometimes we're afraid to ask God questions, thinking such a practice is irreverent or risky. But the truth is that questions can be holy guides leading us to truth and intimacy with God. In fact, our good God delights in using our uncertainty, curiosity, and even anger to draw us closer to Him. As we begin to view our questions as sacred tools of connection and discovery, God uses them to deepen our faith and lead us to a more fulfilling and hope-filled life.

So, I invite you to jump on board the "tangled faith" struggle bus—if you're not already on it! You're going to be in good company because we all struggle in our faith from time to time. Though our circumstances may be different, the questions we ask when life is difficult, disappointing, or devastating are amazingly similar. The chaos and confusion that come with uncertainty are universal. Together we will explore six common questions that can help us untangle our faith:

1. Can I trust God?
2. How can I grow in my faith?
3. Why should I pray?
4. What must I do to be healed?
5. How can I know God's will?
6. What does it mean to follow God?

We will examine one of these questions each week by looking through the lens of specific questions Jesus asked, allowing His questions to help us

- consider the nature of God,
- explore our own questions with God, and
- reclaim hope as we draw closer to God.

The goal is not to find answers per se, though you're likely to gain more insight and understanding along the way. The real gift is having permission to explore, discover, uncover, and go deeper with God through questioning—alone and with a safe community offering one another love and encouragement.

Each week you'll find a memory verse, introductory comments on the overarching question, and five lessons with the following elements:

- Jesus's Question
- The Question We Ask
- Leaning into the Question
- Leaning into the Scripture
- Leaning into Hope
- A Practical Next Step

Questions for reflection are interspersed throughout each lesson. It is my hope that you will respond to these questions with authenticity and vulnerability, allowing yourself to lean into the loving embrace of God.

Once a week, you will gather with your group to watch a video, discuss your insights and experiences from the week, and pray together. A complete leader guide is available separately, which includes discussion questions, activities, prayer prompts, and video viewer guides. Ideally, you should complete the first week of lessons before the first group session (each video complements the content you explored during the week), but feel free to adapt the format and material as you see fit to best meet the needs of your group.

My prayer is that this study will remind you that even when your faith feels tangled, God loves you, desires you to seek Him, and welcomes your questions.

Jesus promises us, "Ask and it will be given to you; seek and you will find; knock and the door will be opened to you" (Matthew 7:7). I am excited to embark with you on this journey of questioning, wrestling (only spiritually, of course!), and reclaiming our hope as we grow in our knowledge of the goodness and love of God.

Be curious!
Praying for you,

Amberly

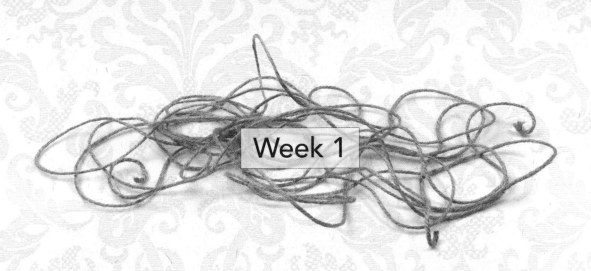

Can I Trust God?

MEMORY VERSE:

*"The Lord is my strength and my shield;
my heart trusts in Him, and He helps me.
My heart leaps for joy,
and with my song I praise Him."*

(Psalm 28:7)

We throw around the word *trust* a lot in our society.

Phrases like "trust fund," "trust me," "trust issues," "living trust," and "a company you can trust" may be part of our everyday vernacular, but saying we trust and actually trusting can be problematic because most of us have had someone (or perhaps lots of someones) breach our trust.

According to *Merriam-Webster*, trust is "assured reliance on the character, ability, strength, or truth of someone or something."¹ This week we will explore the trustworthiness of God by considering His character, His ability, and His strength.

But do not fret, my friend, if you struggle with trust issues when it comes to God, because you are not alone. There are even examples in the Bible of heroes of the faith who struggled with trust.

One such example is John the Baptist, the cousin of Jesus. Through great spiritual commitment—which involved living in the wilderness and baptizing multitudes, including the Messiah Himself—it seemed that his faith in the identity of Jesus was unshakable. But when John was imprisoned, he faced uncertainty and doubt in the trustworthiness of Jesus. John questioned if Jesus was the promised One, asking his followers to inquire of the Lord (Matthew 11:2-15). Though we will not be covering John the Baptist this week, we can certainly empathize with his struggle!

In this first week of *Untangling Faith*, we will address our questions regarding God's trustworthiness as we explore God's nature as a loving parent, His goodness, His faithfulness, His character as a safe place, and His desire for us to see Him clearly. A deep dive into who God is can be the first step to unraveling, grappling with, rediscovering, and rebuilding our "trust fund" with God.

Day 1 | God Is a Loving Parent

Big Idea

God responds to our needs as a loving Parent.

Jesus's Question:
*"Which of you fathers, if your son asks for a fish,
will give him a snake instead?"*
(Luke 11:11)

The Question We Ask:
Does God care about me and my struggle?

Leaning into the Question

No one seemed to hear my continued cries for help. The acoustics in the bathroom made my wailing deafening to my ears, but the adjacent rooms were designed so that outside sounds were muffled—because no one heard me.

"HEEEEEEEEEELLLLLP! Please, anyone, help. Scotty?!?!"

My husband, Scott, was sitting with dear friends down the hall in the church. We were having lunch together and discussing ministry, friendship, and the excitement of expecting our first child. I had been pregnant before and had suffered miscarriages, but this time the pregnancy had surpassed the first trimester, and we thought we were home free.

Needing to use the restroom (not unusual for a pregnant lady!), I had made my way through the labyrinth of hallways in this historic church building designed by Frank Lloyd Wright and found myself gawking at the beauty of the architecture. When I finally found the facilities, I hurriedly closed the stall door and shimmied my skirt up. Then I saw the blood. My underwear was spotted with crimson dots, and I knew this was not a good sign. I had felt a little uncomfortable earlier that day but had excused it as the effects of something I had eaten, never thinking that my unborn baby was in danger.

For many years, we had begged, cajoled, and bargained with God for a child. I had cried more tears, said more prayers, consulted with more doctors, read more books, thrown more fits, and tried more fertility techniques than one could count. Our hearts had leapt with joy when the baby first leapt in my womb. We had already lost our hearts to this unborn stranger. We had been discussing baby names every night for years, and now we were decorating the nursery and

purchasing clothes for this long-awaited answer to our prayers. We had *plans*. But in the moments that followed, my body expelled our precious child along with our hopes, our dreams, and our plans.

I began to weep, quietly at first, but then I realized that I wanted someone to hear me—just as I wanted to know that God heard my cries for help, even though I felt alone. *I'm in a church, for goodness sake, I thought to myself, it should be a safe place to cry and mourn.* So, I began to wail. I wanted my husband to find me, mourn with me, hold me, and tell me that everything would be alright.

But it wasn't alright.

That was a long time ago. Since that loss, we have had two children, who have grown into amazing adults. We have been married over thirty years and have rich, fulfilling lives. Weeks go by when I do not think of the baby we lost, but sometimes the loss comes rushing back—as it did one day recently.

A small bird was nesting in the awning of our front porch. Our family watched her build the nest, and then we watched each morning as she nurtured and protected the eggs in that nest. It was a joy to watch, indeed. But one morning, we woke to find that the nest had been knocked over, likely by a predator on the hunt, causing the eggs to fall onto the concrete floor of our porch. The splattered shards of eggshell and yellow tint of lingering yolk represented the dashed hopes of that mama bird.

In the following days, she would flap and squawk at the place where the nest once had been. We had removed the nest and cleaned the porch to the best of our ability, but the faintest hints of the mama bird's loss are still visible on the concrete months later; I am not sure they will ever disappear completely.

I understand that all too well. You probably do, too.

Maybe you've lost a job, a spouse, a child, a friend, a dream, or an opportunity somewhere down the line, and you want to tell that mama bird that it will be alright. She will make other nests, fly other days, and enjoy other sunrises. But you know that the sting of loss never goes away completely.

Name three losses that you have suffered.

1.

2.

3.

When and how did God seem near and present in those losses?
When and how did God seem distant or absent?

Did those losses shake your confidence in His love in any way? If so, how?

How have those losses shaped you and your understanding of God's love? Would you say they have grown you or made you stronger? Explain your response.

The days following the miscarriage were filled with family and friends who encircled us and loved us well. But if I am honest, they also were filled with questions for God. *Why would You allow this to happen? What did we do to deserve this? Are You mad at us? Can You be trusted?*

Trust in God is a hallmark of the Christian faith. But trust in God is honed and developed through difficulties, challenges, and all manner of experiences over time as God meets our needs. Along the way, those experiences may leave us asking: *Is God good?* Fortunately for us who are looking for answers, Jesus asked his followers some questions that provide insight into the character of God.

Leaning into the Scripture

In the opening verses of Luke 11, Jesus teaches His followers about prayer, offers an analogy, and asks several questions of them. Verse 1 reads,

> *One day Jesus was praying in a certain place. When he finished, one of his disciples said to him, "Lord, teach us to pray, just as John taught his disciples."*

I think it is so fitting that this chapter, in which Jesus addresses an unspoken question through even more questions, begins with a bit of ambiguity. Luke writes, "One day...in a certain place." He does not disclose the specific day or name the exact location where Jesus and His disciples are. Just as this leaves us with unanswered questions, so there are unanswered questions in our lives. Sometimes, we struggle with the concept of God being loving and good because we are uncertain about something that has or hasn't happened in our lives.

The next sentence is key. One of the disciples—yet another ambiguity, for no specific name is given—asks Jesus for help with prayer. The disciples knew how to pray, so essentially, he is wanting to know how to talk with God in order to know Him better. Jesus responds with the Lord's Prayer. This prayer that is often recited in worship, prayed alone and in groups, sung in weddings, and taught to children gives us a glimpse into some characteristics of God. Let's look at each line of the prayer and peek into the keyhole, so to speak, to see God's nature. (Comments about God's nature are added within brackets.)

> ²*He said to them, "When you pray, say: 'Father, hallowed be your name, our kingdom come.* [God is holy, and He reigns.] ³*Give us each day our daily bread.* [God is a provider.] ⁴*Forgive us our sins, for we also forgive everyone who sins against us.* [God is forgiving.] *And lead us not into temptation.* [God is stronger than anything that tempts us.]'"
>
> (Luke 11:2-4)

A few verses later, Jesus reveals more of God's love as He makes a promise and provides hope for those who are eager to truly know God. (Comments regarding God's nature are added within brackets.)

> ⁹*"So I say to you: Ask and it will be given to you; seek and you will find; knock and the door will be opened to you.* [God can be known and will provide for all our needs.] ¹⁰*For everyone who asks receives; the one who seeks finds; and to the one who knocks, the door will be opened.* [God welcomes everyone who seeks Him.]
>
> (Luke 11:9-10)

Then Jesus turns the table on those listening and, instead of stating truths, begins to use one of His favorite tactics for sparking thought: questions. Even in these questions, Jesus continues to reveal the love of God. (Comments regarding God's nature are added within brackets.)

> ¹¹*"Which of you fathers, if your son asks for a fish, will give him a snake instead?* [God is a loving parent.] ¹²*Or if he asks for an egg, will give him a scorpion?* [God hears and responds lovingly to our pleas.] ¹³*If you then, though you are evil, know how to give good gifts to your children, how much more will your Father in heaven give the Holy Spirit to those who ask him!"* [God desires to give us everything we need.]
>
> (Luke 11:11-13)

As Jesus poses these questions, He is not just addressing His closest followers. He is posing these questions for all who would seek Him throughout the years to come—that includes me and you. He is revealing clues about the nature of our loving God in these questions and allowing us the opportunity to ponder how we see God.

How do you see God? What is your image of God in this season of life?

How has your image of God changed through the years?

If I'm honest, there have been times when I've questioned the love of God—times when I have prayed and what occurs seems more like a scorpion than an egg. But as I have grown in my understanding of God's character, I have realized that God does not give me bad gifts. God is a loving Parent who longs to meet the needs of His children. And in those times when bad things happen, He redeems them, including giving us the gift of understanding Him better.

A pastor friend of mine has the opportunity to visit those from his congregation who are hospitalized. On one occasion, he visited an elderly lady from his church—I will call her Lois—the day she was scheduled to be released. She told him that she had encouraged many of the doctors and nurses, praying and sharing Jesus with some of them. Lois felt she had made a difference while there.

Soon after their visit, her son helped her into a wheelchair and began to push her toward the parking lot to make their way home. On the way to the car, a vehicle speeding through the parking lot clipped her wheelchair, causing Lois to fall and hit the sidewalk, sustaining injuries.

My pastor friend, who had gone to visit another church member in a different wing of the hospital, heard the commotion outside but did not know it involved Lois. Later, on his way to the hospital exit, he heard a familiar voice call out, "Pastor, I guess I'll have more time here to pray and encourage the staff."

I guess if you are going to be hit by a car, the parking lot of the hospital is not the worst place! As unfortunate as Lois's accident was, she was able to see God's loving provision in providing for her care and continuing to use her in a powerful way while in the hospital. God gave her peace and comfort despite her new injuries. He encouraged her by letting her know that she could continue to accomplish valuable things there, including speaking through her as she shared the good news with her new hospital roommate, who came to faith in Jesus.

> God is a loving Parent who longs to meet the needs of His children.

Only in retrospect could Lois clearly see that God was busy "working all things for good" (Romans 8:28)—for her good and His glory—even a car accident! That's usually the case in our lives as well. But we can grow in our ability to trust God until our vision becomes clearer. We can trust God because God responds to our needs as a loving parent.

Think of a time in your life when you experienced a tragedy, travesty, or trauma. It might be one of the losses you wrote about earlier. What questions did you have for God then?

What was it like to wrestle with those questions with God? Have any of those questions been answered? If so, how? What questions remain?

Has God demonstrated to you that He sees your needs and "it's going to be OK"? If so, how? If you're unsure, what do you want God to know? Write your prayer below.

While your life may not have turned out as you envisioned or planned, in what ways can you see the loving-kindness of God in your life today?

A Practical Next Step

Pray the Lord's Prayer each day this week. Focus on whichever line stands out to you that day and offer thanks to God for that quality of His character (see page 14)—or ask God to open your eyes to that quality of His character in the ordinary events of your day. Begin to look for evidence of God's loving-kindness and care in your everyday life.

Day 2 | God Is Good

Jesus's Question:
"You of little faith, why are you talking among yourselves about having no bread? Do you still not understand?"
(Matthew 16:8-9a)

The Question We Ask:
Is everything going to be OK?

Leaning into the Question

The teachers' lounge in any school can be a hotbed of crazy. When overworked, exhausted, frustrated educators are given a few minutes of respite around others in the same situation, it can look a lot more like a complaint center or therapy office than just a place to eat one's lunch. If it has been an especially difficult day (think rainy days when everyone is stuck inside or the last few weeks of school), a gathering of teachers in the lounge can feel like the Avengers assembling rather than coworkers recharging their batteries.

I am not saying that is true of every school, but in the schools where I have worked, the teachers' lounge has been a room I have avoided. Not because I don't need empathy from coworkers or I am too cool for the other employees (I have had the same hairstyle since 1988, so we know that's not true!), but because the discussions about students, especially the challenging ones, always proved troublesome for me. In the past, I sometimes allowed the negative talk about a challenging student to cloud my experience with that student once they made their way to my classroom, so I learned to avoid such conversations at all costs. I want to give everyone a fair shake.

I wish I had done the same thing with comments about God before becoming a Christian. I did not grow up in a home that practiced any type of faith per se, but I inherited some erroneous opinions through the media and conversations with peers regarding God's character, such as:

- God is always angry,
- God is waiting for us to mess up,
- God is vengeful,

- God does not want us to have fun, and
- God only loves us when we are behaving. (I still struggle with this lie.)

Only through many years of following God; reading His Word; learning from people with more mileage on their "faith vehicle"; and experiencing God working in, through, and around—and sometimes despite—me have those erroneous messages dissipated.

What are some of the lies and misperceptions about God that you inherited or learned?

What has helped to open your eyes to the truth about who God is? How would you describe God now?

Which lies do you still struggle with at times? When do you seem to be more susceptible to these lies?

It has taken years to replace the lies I believed about God with the truth of God's character. I still often struggle to give more of my attention to who I am in Jesus than to who I am in relationship to other human beings.

This healing process begins with identifying the lies I have believed and replacing them with truths from God's Word and then rehearsing those truths in my mind and my everyday experience until they are hidden in my heart. It is like a recycling program for my thoughts. I exchange the old lies with truths from God's Word about who God is and who I am, and I invite God to make those truths part of my experiential reality—my lived experience.

Yet sometimes, when I least expect it, I still can hear one of the old lies whispered into my ear by the Enemy. I foolishly give the microphone to past regrets and remnants of early conditioning. When I entertain old lies that stem from past hurts, hang-ups, and habits, I'm allowing those lies to drown out the truths of God's living Word about my real identity and the faithfulness of God.

We can suffer from spiritual amnesia and forget how good God is. We also can have parts of ourselves that still do not know, understand, and trust the goodness of God—often due to emotional wounds that happened early in life. Either way, when we allow ourselves to ruminate on the lies, our faith can begin to unravel.

So, often we find ourselves back at square one, asking ourselves, *Is God good?* This is such a tricky question because in our society, "good" is a harder concept to grasp than a greased pig.

- *How are you?* someone asks. / *I am good,* we answer. (That may not be good grammar, but we still say it!)
- *How is the brisket at this restaurant?* / *It is so good.*
- *What is the weather like in your neck of the woods?* / *It is good.*
- *How was the fundraiser?* / *It was good.*

These questions and responses require the questioner and responder to define for themselves what "good" means. When some people are asked how they are, answering "good" means "I got a lot accomplished" or "The stock exchange was healthy today." For others, it means, "I got out of bed today" or "My parole officer hasn't caught me yet."

But when discussing the goodness of God, there are characteristics from scripture we can use as a reference point:

- perfect in character (Psalm 92:15),
- benevolent (Exodus 34:6; Psalm 34:8),
- graceful (Romans 3:24),
- merciful (Ephesians 2:4),
- just (Psalm 25:8), and
- loving (Psalm 107:8-9).

What other divine characteristics named in scripture would you add to describe God's goodness?

It is one thing to define God's goodness through the truths of God's Word. It is another thing to examine it through the filter of our life experiences.

My wedding day is so vividly and deeply etched in my mind that it feels more like last week than thirty years ago.

Scott and I were paying for our own wedding (for the most part) and "shoestring" does not begin to describe the budget. Scott's grandmother did the flowers, his dad officiated our ceremony (yes, I married a pastor's kid), his aunt made my veil, we got married in his home church (being the pastor's kid has its privileges!), and our friends provided most of the music.

A very popular part of weddings in the 1990s was to have a song in the middle of the ceremony. We wanted to sing to each other. Yes, both of us sing (although he sings much better than I do), but we both knew that our emotions would not allow us to do so live. I knew I would be a blubbering idiot when I got going, so we thought it best to record the song. We could not afford a recording studio, so we used a tape recorder. (If you are too young to know what that is, you can Google it!) We got two recordings of the song—one was fair and the other was the one we would use for the ceremony.

When we came to that part of the wedding ceremony and the music started, people started to look around to see who was going to sing. My soon-to-be husband (like, six minutes from then soon-to-be) looked me in the eyes and whispered, "The tape got mangled, but it's OK. I fixed it enough to play the other version." My face bunched up. "It is going to be OK," he assured me, and as if I hadn't heard it the first time, he repeated, "It's going to be OK."

I wish I could say that I felt like everything was going to be OK. My husband is cute, and I wanted to trust him, but he does not know the future. In the months to follow, everything did not seem OK—I still couldn't seem to get pregnant, fit into my skinny jeans, stop overeating bread, or bring world peace. But God continued to draw me to His heart. As He did, I started to see more clearly that things are not going to be OK because circumstances will miraculously improve. Things are not going to be OK because I get what I ask for in prayer. Things are going to be OK because God is good. Period.

Scott has said "It's going to be OK" ten thousand times or more since we got married. Finances, kids, safety, friendships, infertility, broken appliances, the death of parents, and lost jobs are just a few of the splotches on the canvas of our marriage, times when Scott has assured me with the words "It's going to be OK." I learned to believe him—not because Scott is good or I am good, but because the words point us to the good character of God, who can be trusted.

Scott and I have covered a lot of mileage on our faith journey together, and we can remind each other that "It's going to be OK" because we know we "will see the goodness of the Lord in the land of the living" (Psalm 27:13). Faith can be fostered in churches, in prayer, and in

scripture, but it also can be strengthened in times of despair and uncertainty—when we feel that we are at the end of our rope and our hope.

Through heartache, loss, disappointment, and fear, God has proven Himself faithful to me, as I'm sure He has for you. That does not mean we do not have questions at times, but if we will recall the faithfulness He has shown us in the past—even when we cannot see it clearly in the present—we will be strengthened and reassured. And should a time be so devastating that we are unable even to recall God's faithfulness, we can lean upon our sisters and brothers in Christ to uphold us by their faith until we're strengthened once again to believe "It's going to be OK" because of God's goodness.

Even the most faithful followers of Jesus can sometimes struggle with "spiritual amnesia"—temporarily forgetting all that God has done and has been. When that occurs, we need a holy refresher course by digging into God's Word.

> Even the most faithful followers of Jesus can sometimes struggle with "spiritual amnesia."

Leaning into the Scripture

Jesus's right-hand men had front-row seats to healings, exorcisms of demons, and resurrections from the dead—all displaying God's power and purpose through Jesus. They listened as He taught people about the love of His Father. They saw Jesus feed thousands with amazing amounts of leftovers—baskets full of bread illustrating God's provision. Yet, somehow they missed the consistent, albeit unspoken, message of Jesus: "Trust me. It's going to be OK."

A conversation between the apostles about some of the religious leaders of the day, the Pharisees and Sadducees, incited a question-a-palooza from Jesus. Like a tennis ball machine, Jesus peppered His disciples with questions that got to the heart of their lack of faith and their amnesia regarding the way God had provided for them.

> [8]Aware of their discussion, Jesus asked, "You of little faith, why are you talking among yourselves about having no bread? [9]Do you still not understand? Don't you remember the five loaves for the five thousand, and how many basketfuls you gathered? [10]Or the seven loaves for the four thousand, and how many basketfuls you gathered? [11]How is it you don't understand that I was not talking to you about bread? But be on your guard against the yeast of the Pharisees and Sadducees." [12]Then they understood that he was not telling them to guard against the yeast used in bread, but against the teaching of the Pharisees and Sadducees.
>
> (Matthew 16:8-12)

Jesus asked these questions about bread faster than my family can power through a basket of breadsticks from Olive Garden—but I think the questions pertain more to the goodness of His Father than to actual bread! Through these questions,

Jesus points out the lack of faith on the part of the disciples and paints a vivid and compelling picture of the character and goodness of God.

One commentator notes that when Jesus said, "You of little faith," He was communicating that the disciples shouldn't worry about the provision of their needs:

> They should not have supposed, after the miracles that he had performed in feeding so many, that he would caution them to be anxious about procuring bread for their necessities. It was improper, then, for them to reason about a thing like that, but they should have supposed that he referred to something more important. The miracles had been full proof that he could supply all their wants without such anxiety.[2]

In other words, they had seen Jesus provide in a miraculous way, so why would they doubt now?

We could certainly read this passage as Jesus packing the bags of the disciples for a major guilt trip, but instead, I think we should look at it as a glimpse into Jesus's desire to emphasize the faithfulness of God.

Let's break down what Jesus is saying through His questions.

- *"You of little faith"* (v. 8).
  Jesus calls out His disciples on their lack of trust in God.

- *"Why are you talking among yourselves about having no bread? Do you still not understand?"* (vv. 8-9a).
  Instead of encouraging one another and discussing the faithfulness that God has shown them—a group of men who have been traveling, eating, and living without jobs for the past three years—they are focusing on what they do not have instead of what they do have.

- *"Don't you remember the five loaves for the five thousand, and how many basketfuls you gathered? Or the seven loaves for the four thousand, and how many basketfuls you gathered? How is it you don't understand that I was not talking to you about bread?"* (vv. 9-11).
  Jesus is calling the disciples to recall the miracles that God has done in their lives and live accordingly. He is calling them to recognize that God has shown His character of goodness to them clearly and practically.

Sometimes, when we are questioning the goodness of God, it is because we are failing to take our eyes off the present circumstances long enough to recall and recount what He has done for us in the past—to remember the faith mileage we have with Him—for our own sake and the sake of others.

Leaning into Hope

Taking time to recall the goodness of God becomes easier to do once we replace erroneous information about who God is with the truth of God's character—found in scripture and supported by the evidence of God's goodness in our lives.

For years, I have kept a journal to recount all the amazing things God has done. It is a great way to recall His character and take my eyes off the current circumstances. Although He does good things because of His goodness every day in my life, I am not as faithful to chronicle all of them in my journal. But looking back on my journals I have kept for decades does serve as a reminder of the good works God does; and when I waver in my faith, those journals become annuals of God's goodness.

Another way to notice the evidence of God's goodness in our lives is to review our day before going to bed, remembering the moments when we experienced or observed the goodness and love of God. As we allow simple, everyday experiences to "bubble up," we can receive them as gifts from our good Father, reminding ourselves, "Every good and perfect gift is from above, coming down from the Father of the heavenly lights, who does not change like shifting shadows" (James 1:17).

Sharing with a prayer partner, accountability partner, spiritual companion, or discipleship group is yet another way to recount the goodness of God. Others can help us to see God's activity in our lives that we otherwise might miss or overlook, as well as allow us to affirm and confirm evidence of God's loving-kindness toward us.

Whatever helps us to notice and recall the goodness of God, we can be sure that the more we focus on the goodness of God instead of the ugliness of the world, the greater our hope will be! God will be faithful to demonstrate His goodness in our everyday lives.

Here are a few questions to help you lean into hope as you contemplate God's goodness in your everyday life.

What are some practices or habits in your life that help you remember God's goodness? How are they bolstering your trust in God?

Choose one of the challenges you are currently facing and listen for what God has to say to you about it. What would it look like for you to trust God in this situation? Where can you identify the goodness of God in this situation?

What are some ways you have seen God work in your life in the past? How is God inviting you to trust Him in this season? Is there something God is inviting you to consider, do, or become?

List ten ways you see God's good provision in your life right now.

1.

2.

3.

4.

5.

6.

7.

8.

9.

10.

Finish this phrase, "If I truly understood how good God is and how much He loves me, I would/would not _____."

How does worry take your eyes off Jesus? How can you release your cares and refocus your gaze on Jesus? What happens to your worry when you do this?

A Practical Next Step

Make a list of what you are thankful for in your life, noting why each is a good gift of God. Gratitude turns on the relational circuits of the brain, which enable us to feel safe and build trust. By giving thanks, you are reminding yourself of God's goodness, deepening your relationship, and increasing your trust in Him.

Day 3 God Is Faithful

Jesus's Question:
"Can any one of you by worrying add a single hour to your life?"
(Matthew 6:27)

The Question We Ask:
What's going to happen?

Big Idea

God is faithful to take care of all that concerns me.

Leaning into the Question

As I write this, I am waiting for my skin cancer tests to return. Just days ago, my dermatologist removed a small chunk of my back to send in for testing. My dad died of skin cancer at the age of fifty-one, so it gave me lots to think about at age fifty-two.

Now, I wait. With every phone call, message, and email, there is a side-order of dread. I self-diagnose my illness and begin a mental train of thought that completely derails me.

How will Scott make house payments without my income?
Where will he and the kids live?
How will this affect their spiritual lives?
Will they be mad at God for letting me die?

But then, I am back to reality. My logic kicks back in, and I talk myself off the ledge by making true statements about the situation.

The chances of dying are slim.
Medical advances have made great strides.
I am blessed to live in a time with incredible technology.
As I rehearse these truths, I feel my heart rate slow, and I take a deep breath. The peace lasts only a minute before I am back on the same crazy train.

Technology costs a lot. So do hospital bills. How will we ever pay for my recovery?

Will we lose the house?
Will we be able to spend time with our grandkids? (We don't even have grandkids yet!)
Will we lose any hope of retiring before we both die from exhaustion? (Wow, it got morbid quickly!)

Although the test results came back negative for cancer, the damage of my worry and stress did damage to my heart and mind.

When we face uncertainties, questions can serve as a healthy tool to help us process what we are going through, but only when the questions are grounded in the truth of God and His character can they transition us from panicked questioning to peace.

Do you have a particular challenge that is plaguing your thoughts right now? If so, what is it?

What questions related to this challenge run through your mind repeatedly?

Are these questions grounded in the truth of God and His character?

God is bigger than skin cancer. He has never promised that I will not have skin cancer, but He does promise throughout scripture to be with me, no matter the diagnosis or circumstance. God is bigger than the heartache of rebellious children, lost jobs, aging parents, crashing stock markets, car problems, organizational buyouts, bickering in the church, doubt, disappointment, disillusionment, and stressful diagnoses.

Whatever is taking up bandwidth in your mind and heart right now, you can trust God with it. Even when it feels scary and uncertain, He can be trusted.

Leaning into the Scripture

In Matthew 5, Jesus is preaching to thousands of men, women, and children in His most recognizable sermon, the Sermon on the Mount. He is giving His followers practical wisdom and instructions for life, often using the "props" around Him to articulate the lessons, including birds that may have been flying overhead at the time. These birds were beautiful examples of the care of God.

> [25]"Therefore I tell you, do not worry about your life, what you will eat or drink; or about your body, what you will wear. Is not life more than food, and the body more than clothes? [26]Look at the birds of the air; they do not sow or reap or store away in barns, and yet your heavenly Father feeds them. Are you not much more valuable than they? [27]Can any one of you by worrying add a single hour to your life?"
>
> (Matthew 6:25-27)

This series of questions is mind-boggling and faith stirring. It is a rapid succession of powerful, gut-wrenching, heart status–type questions. I don't know about you, but maybe some mind-boggling and faith stirring are exactly what I need to get my train of thought off my fears and back where it belongs!

I love that Jesus prefaces the trust question—"Can any one of you by worrying add a single hour to your life?"—with the value question: "Are you not much more valuable than they?"

As we truly embrace just how much God loves us and allow that love to heal and transform us (which is a process that happens over time), we become less inclined to say and do things that cause harm to ourselves and to others.

As we come to know and believe we are beloved children of God, we become less likely to seek affection, approval, comfort, or courage through people and activities we know aren't good for us—and more likely to reach out for help when we find ourselves in trouble.

As we come to know and embrace the grace and forgiveness of God, we're not as prone to say hurtful things or condemn the behavior of others, especially on social media where it's easy to hide behind a screen.

As we begin to realize how fearfully and wonderfully we are made and experience how much our Creator delights in us, we're less likely to mistreat ourselves and practice self-loathing.

But along this journey of transformation—and despite the fact that we know Jesus died on the cross for us—we still hurt others, devalue ourselves, and forget that we are valuable to God.

Knowing this, Jesus is both assuring and reassuring his listeners when he asks the question "Are you not much more valuable than they?" He wants the people to know that they are precious in the eyes of the One who made them, shaped them,

When we face uncertainties, questions can serve as a healthy tool to help us process what we are going through, but only when the questions are grounded in the truth of God and His character.

gave them life, breathed air into their lungs, and—out of His great love—provides for them.

Right after the reminder of our value, Jesus gently—or perhaps not so gently—reminds us of the corrosive power of worry: "Can any one of you by worrying add a single hour to your life?" Worry takes our eyes off Him.

If we were to examine what we worry about most, it might serve as a litmus test of our faith. Where we worry is probably a good indicator of what we treasure and where we put our hope.

Leaning into Hope

When I hear Jesus's question, my mind goes straight to our house. We bought a house a few years ago, and I love it. I know that it was a bit of a stretch for us, but I feel so blessed that God has given us the opportunity to live there. But whenever finances get tight, my mind goes directly—do not pass Go and do not collect $200—to whether we will be able to make the house payment at all.

My mouth says my hope is in the Lord, but my worry communicates otherwise. If I truly believed in my heart of hearts that God values me and my family, I would trust that He will provide a place for us even if we were to lose the house.

Jesus's question gets to the heart of the matter for me, reminding me that God is good even when my trust in Him is weak. He is faithful, even when my faith wavers. He is love, even when I do not love how things are turning out from my perspective. How about you? How does Jesus's question get at the heart of the matter for you?

Where does your mind go first when you hear Jesus's question: "Can any one of you by worrying add a single hour to your life"? Do you think of the challenge you named earlier or something else?

What do the things you worry about reveal about (1) what you treasure, and (2) where you put your hope?

How do you see evidence of the faithfulness of God in your life and in the world?

Jesus asked a probing question that day to the followers on that hillside, and He asks the same question to you and me: "Can any one of you by worrying add a single hour to your life?" (Matthew 6:27).

- It is probing because it is personal: "Can any one of you . . ."?
- It is probing because it is pointed: ". . . by worrying"? Worry is something most of us struggle with!
- It is probing because it is perspective-giving: ". . . add a single hour to your life"?

His question gets to the heart of our matter—the desire to control. God has dominion over all the areas where worry can creep in. He is omnipresent (always present), omniscient (all-knowing), and omnipotent (all-powerful). He created all things, including time and each of us, and He is the only one who has supremacy over life and time. Choosing to trust Him dissipates our worries and brings great relief. God will be faithful to take care of all that concerns you and me.

A Practical Next Step

Make a "worry list" of the things plaguing your thoughts right now. Beside each worry, write a statement about God's faithful love and provision. Include a promise from scripture if you like. Offer each worry to God by imagining it flying into the heavens as a bird. Then, rather than praying about your worries, offer prayers of thanks for how God is going to meet your needs. If you are feeling especially "artistic," feel free to draw a little bird above the statement about God's faithful love and provision as a gentle reminder.

Day 4 God Is My Safe Place

Big Idea

God is my refuge, especially when things are falling apart.

Jesus's Question:
"Don't you know me?"
(John 14:9)

The Question We Ask:
Will God keep me safe?

Leaning into the Question

Most of the kids I have known go through a "season." They have a train season, a car season, a doll season, a LEGO season, or some other season—a period of time when they are obsessed with a certain theme, character, TV show, toy, or concept.

My kids also went through seasons. My son, Josiah, went through a particularly uncommon season—a *Titanic* season. For over a year in his life, he read everything he could about the fateful sinking of the British passenger liner and its passengers. It may seem morose that a six-year-old was intrigued with a White Star Line vessel that sank in 1912, but he has always had a fascination with engineering, and the story of the *Titanic* still baffles engineers and scientists alike. Josiah even purchased the largest LEGO set to date, a replica of the *Titanic*, as his first purchase with money he earned from work just over a year ago. So, maybe this season is not quite over for him; it is still a source of joy and discovery.

But not everyone agrees with Josiah's assessment.

For some, the series of events on April 15, 1912, are devastating. Of the 706 survivors, Millvina Dean was the last living witness to the *Titanic* shipwreck. She was approximately two months old when she and her family boarded the famous ocean liner; and although she was too young to remember the tragedy of its sinking, she became the youngest of the 706 survivors. Her mother and her brother, Bertram, also survived on a lifeboat, but her father died in the wreck as he stayed aboard the ship.

The family returned to England where she participated in *Titanic*-related programs, activities, and events through the years. But after the 1958 film *A Night to Remember* proved too much

for her emotionally, she avoided all media depictions of the *Titanic*, including the blockbuster film in 1997. She was willing to share her experiences with anyone who cared to listen, but she was unwilling to watch the events of that fateful night unfold on the big screen. In 2003 she was invited to a documentary about the mighty ship, but she politely declined.

In 1997, the year the movie *Titanic* was released, Millvina was sponsored by the Titanic Historical Society to visit Kansas City for a commemorative event there. But sadly, there was not a lot of money in being a *Titanic* survivor. While many profited handsomely from the film, Millvina was in dire financial straits. In 2009, to pay off nursing home bills, she auctioned off personal artifacts from the *Titanic* sinking.

A personal friend of Millvina was moved by her situation and contacted the main players of the film for help. Much to the surprise of many, his efforts paid off. The two main actors, Kate Winslet and Leonardo DiCaprio, along with the movie's director, James Cameron, gave a combined $30,000 to a fund established on behalf of Millvina.

Millvina was blown away by their generosity. Unfortunately, soon after receiving their financial support, she fell ill from pneumonia and never recovered. She passed away at the age of ninety-seven on May 31, 2009—exactly ninety-eight years to the day that the *Titanic* was launched from Belfast.[3]

Though the *Titanic* was the source of great heartache for Millvina and her family, it was the vehicle that provided for her financially at the end of her life. Though her earthly father perished aboard the ship, her heavenly Father never left her side. Though God did not promise her smooth sailing through life, He was with her all ninety-seven years on earth. Though God did not spare her from financial hardship, He met her needs with comfort and provision.

In a sense, God redeemed Millvina's story, allowing her pain ultimately to lead to her provision—and my hope is that God's provision for Millvina included the comfort of knowing she was not forgotten but cared for and loved. I pray she had eyes to see that through all she endured, God was her refuge, her safe place.

Our good God is always with us, our safe place in the midst of life's storms and the One who

redeems our stories. But it doesn't always seem that way in the moment, does it? Sometimes we feel as if we are drowning in our circumstances, causing us to wonder if God is working in our best interests—if He cares about our struggles and is protecting us in our present situation.

When have you doubted God's protection? Why?

When have you been certain of the protection of God? Why?

I have taught both junior high and college students for decades, but I had a stint as a long-term substitute at a local high school when I was pregnant with my daughter—and teaching high school students was an amazing experience. I had an office, which is a bit unusual for a teacher; but because I did not have a classroom of my own, the administration thought it best to assign me my own space to work from.

One day after a long afternoon of teaching, I went into my office for a break (I was pregnant after all). As I went to sit in my office chair, I realized I was not alone—not because of my child in utero but because someone else was under my desk! I screamed, recognizing that I startled the student more than he scared me.

When I asked for an explanation (after my heart rate returned to normal), he said he was just looking for a safe place to hide from a mean teacher. He had had a particularly challenging day with one of his instructors and just wanted to find a place of safety to hide until the bell rang.

There are certainly days I look for refuge when I am feeling unsafe. I think everyone can relate to needing a place of safety in the midst of a challenging day or circumstance. Some people, even those of us who are believers, find solace and safety in food, drink, the arms of another, drugs, a good romance novel, busyness, perfectionism, or music; but God is the only Safe Place that truly satisfies. When life doesn't feel safe, we can find security in knowing we are safe in the arms of God.

Where do you tend to go first when you need a safe place?

Do you consider God a safe place for you right now, in this season?
Why or why not?

Leaning into the Scripture

In John 14, Jesus is talking with His disciples and trying to
encourage them by answering their questions. Thomas
(yes, the doubting guy) and Philip ask Jesus questions,
and I love that we have this glimpse of their interaction;
it gives me such comfort when I myself have questions
for God.

> ⁵Thomas said to him, "Lord, we don't know
> where you are going, so how can we know
> the way?"
>
> ⁶Jesus answered, "I am the way and the
> truth and the life. No one comes to the Father
> except through me. ⁷If you really know me, you will know my Father as
> well. From now on, you do know him and have seen him."
>
> ⁸Philip said, "Lord, show us the Father and that will be enough for us."
>
> ⁹Jesus answered: "**Don't you know me, Philip**, even after I have been
> among you such a long time? Anyone who has seen me has seen the
> Father. How can you say, 'Show us the Father'? ¹⁰Don't you believe that
> I am in the Father, and that the Father is in me? The words I say to you I
> do not speak on my own authority. Rather, it is the Father, living in me,
> who is doing his work. ¹¹Believe me when I say that I am in the Father
> and the Father is in me; or at least believe on the evidence of the works
> themselves. ¹²Very truly I tell you, whoever believes in me will do the
> works I have been doing, and they will do even greater things than these,
> because I am going to the Father. ¹³And I will do whatever you ask in my
> name, so that the Father may be glorified in the Son. ¹⁴You may ask me for
> anything in my name, and I will do it."
>
> (John 14:5-14, emphasis added)

Jesus answers Philip's questions by appealing to their connection as friends. Philip
had walked hundreds of miles, literally and figuratively, with Jesus in the three years
of ministry. Philip had seen Jesus do amazing things, yet he had doubts.

Philip also had been with Jesus when things were less than amazing—feeling pressure from the religious leaders of the day (Mark 3:2-4); encountering an angry mob with weapons (Matthew 26:47-54); enduring controversy (Matthew 9:10-13); and watching their leader, mentor, and friend die on a cross (Luke 23:26-49), just to name a few.

Philip endured great hardships—just as Millvina, the *Titanic* survivor, did. Rather than be defeated by these hardships, he survived, just as Millvina did, and he grew stronger—going on to do "greater things than [the works of Jesus]" (John 14:12). How? Because God was his safe place. God carried him through the difficulties because of His great love.

With that in mind, let us unpack the question of Jesus to Philip in this passage: "Don't you know me?" In other words, haven't you learned by now that I am your safe place, Philip? I'd like to highlight four things that stand out to me from Jesus's words in this passage.

> God does not shield us from difficulties in this world, but He does want to be our safe place when the difficulties come.

1. **Know:** "Don't you <u>know</u> me, Philip, even after I have been among you such a long time?" (v. 9)
2. **See:** "Anyone who has <u>seen</u> me has seen the Father." (v. 9)
3. **Believe:** "<u>Believe</u> me when I say that I am in the Father and the Father is in me; or at least believe on the evidence of the works themselves." (v. 11)
4. **Act:** "Very truly I tell you, whoever believes in me will <u>do</u> the works I have been doing, and they will do even greater things than these, because I am going to the Father." (v. 12)

This often is the progression when we desire to grow in our faith: we know, see, believe, and act. When we have more questions than certainty, this pattern can serve us well in becoming the faithful people God desires us to be. What does this look like, practically speaking?

1. **Know:** Continue to seek the truth of who God is. "You will seek me and find me when you seek me with all your heart" (Jeremiah 29:13).
2. **See:** Pay attention to the ways God is at work in your life and the lives of others (including those in the Bible).
3. **Believe:** Choose to trust. Faith is a choice.
4. **Act:** Put into practice the things you are learning about how Jesus loved and served others and watch your faith blossom.

What does it mean for you to make God your "safe place"?

Do you find comfort in the fact that Jesus answered the questions of His disciples? Why or why not? What does this say about who He is?

Which of the four steps or components of a growing faith—know, see, believe, act—is easiest for you to practice? Which is most challenging?

How can these four steps help us in difficult times when we're in need of a safe place?

Leaning into Hope

You and I may not have known the heartbreak of surviving the sinking of an ocean liner, but we have endured our own set of trials, tragedies, travesties, and traumas. Do our stories work out exactly the way they do in movies? Hardly. Are we promised a storybook ending? Nope. Can God work the very hardest parts of our stories into narratives that glorify Him and make us stronger? You betcha He can! Does He give us the freedom to ask questions and wrestle in faith and prayer at the same time? Indeed!

You and I also may not have experienced persecution from religious leaders, mob attacks, or controversy, but we certainly have had an encounter with the cross of Jesus. Even though we were not in Golgotha on that day, we have read and heard accounts of the death, burial, and resurrection of Jesus. And we have been given the opportunity to choose whether or not to follow Jesus and make Him our safe place in the midst of our challenges. God does not shield us from difficulties in this world, but He does want to be our safe place when the difficulties come. We can count on God to be a refuge for us—especially when things are falling apart.

Think of a titanic challenge you have faced in your life. Did you struggle to see God's protection in the midst of that challenge? If so, how?

Looking back, can you see any evidence of God's protection now? Have any good things come from that challenge? Explain your responses.

Where in your life do you see God working on your behalf now?

Where do you need God's protection and safety right now, in this season? Talk with God about it and listen for God's loving response. How are you being invited to exhibit trust in God and allow Him to be your safe place?

A Practical Next Step

Whenever I struggle to trust God's protection and provision, I use the BOAT assessment, which is a tool I created to help filter my thoughts with God in prayer:

- **B** Do I BELIEVE that God is working in my best interest? Why or why not?
- **O** Am I being intentional to OBSERVE ways that God is protecting, providing for, and loving me? What can I notice today?
- **A** Do my ACTIONS reflect my belief that God is working on my behalf? If not, what do I need to share with God, and what do I need from God?
- **T** Am I practicing THANKFULNESS for the things God has done? What am I thankful for today?

Day 5 | God Desires to Help Us See Clearly

Jesus's Question:
"Do you see anything?"
(Mark 8:23)

The Question We Ask:
Will God complete the work He has begun in me?

Leaning into the Question

I am huge fan of chicken fried steak. I don't love gravy (crazy, I know, especially for a Texan). However, I do love some deep-fried goodness. I also love the dives and diners that often serve such a dish. No one eats chicken fried steak for its nutritional benefits. Most of us eat it because of its taste—and perhaps the atmosphere of the establishment.

Let's be honest—you can bread and deep-fry pretty much anything and it tastes good. Twinkies? Sure. Okra? You bet! A briefcase? Probably. But steak? Absolutely!

A restaurant by my folks' house in Texas is just one of those amazing food places that not only serves chicken fried steak but also a great experience to go with it. The place is decorated with all sorts of local paraphernalia—sports awards, town history, and even a deer head (I assume it was a local "find" just like the others on the wall).

When we visited the restaurant one day years ago, the hostess greeted us with a smile as wide as the state and an accent as thick as the gravy they serve. Quickly discerning that my family of four was visiting, she asked my children—Josiah, age three, and Judah, age six—questions about themselves, such as their ages, where we come from, and so forth.

What I did not know is that she passed that information on to the owner, who made the most of it. Halfway through our meal, one of the stuffed deer on the wall came to life. Its eyes got wide, and its mouth opened enough to speak to my kids by *name*. He welcomed us to the restaurant and the town. My kids were mesmerized and squealed with delight.

About a minute in, something happened, however. I do not know what behooved my daughter to do this, but she started to look around to see who was operating the deer. She scanned the

restaurant for someone on a microphone, and when she spotted him, she looked right at me. I smiled, put my finger on my mouth to signal her to be silent, and then pointed at her brother, who obviously was convinced that a deer was talking to him. She was delighted that she and I had a secret.

On the way home, Josiah could not stop talking about the deer. Judah was uncharacteristically quiet but smiling. She had figured out the secret of the talking deer. She had seen the wizard behind the curtain. She was enlightened. She had discovered the truth, something deeper than the "reality" in front of her. But for the sake of her brother, she played along about the magic deer.

Can you recall a time when you came to see the truth of something deeper than the "reality" in front of you? What opened your eyes? How did you feel and respond in that moment?

Sometimes, our perceptions of God and truth become increasingly clear, just as the vision of a blind man in Bethsaida became increasingly clear.

Leaning into the Scripture

Bethsaida—which was the hometown of the apostles Simon Peter, Philip, and Andrew—was near the shore of Galilee. When Jesus and the disciples reached the town, some people brought a blind man to Jesus and begged Him to heal the man of his visual impairment. We find the story in Mark 8:

> [22]*They came to Bethsaida, and some people brought a blind man and begged Jesus to touch him.* [23]*He took the blind man by the hand and led him outside the village. When he had spit on the man's eyes and put his hands on him, Jesus asked, "Do you see anything?"*
>
> [24]*He looked up and said, "I see people; they look like trees walking around."*
>
> [25]*Once more Jesus put his hands on the man's eyes. Then his eyes were opened, his sight was restored, and he saw everything clearly.* [26]*Jesus sent him home, saying, "Don't even go into the village."*
>
> (Mark 8:22-26)

Clearly Jesus had the more active role in this unfolding story. The blind man's actions were more passive, yet he was healed, nonetheless. Jesus healed this man so he

could see for the first time in his life! His eyes were opened, his sight was restored, and he was able to see everything—with blurry vision at first and then clearly. Jesus persisted until the restoration of the man's sight was complete, and he allowed the man to participate in the process. Jesus instructed him what to do, and then He asked, "Do you see anything?" (v. 23). In other words, "What do you see? How is your vision now?"

Jesus does a similar thing in our lives. He touches our spiritual eyes, guides us in next steps, and checks in with us often, asking, "What do you see? How is your vision now?" This process of healing and restoring our spiritual sight continues until it is completed. As we read in Philippians 1:6, "He who began a good work in you will carry it on to completion until the day of Christ Jesus."

This story and Jesus's question, "Do you see anything," give us hope. The man was brought by his friends; he did not even come by himself. But here's what he did do: he allowed himself to be led by Jesus. He allowed himself to be healed (in an unorthodox way, I might add), because he trusted Jesus to do what he couldn't do.

This man did very little—he looked, saw, and spoke—but he desired to see very much. And Jesus healed his vision.

What does this story teach us about the nature of God and trusting God? God is compassionate and desires to heal us! He wants us to see with the eyes of Christ. Though it's a process, we can trust God to complete the healing work He has begun in us. The questions we should ask ourselves in light of this story are, Are we allowing ourselves to be led by God? *Are we trusting Him to heal our spiritual blindness?* Take a moment to answer these questions now.

Are you allowing yourself to be led by God? If so, where is God leading you? If not, what fears, concerns, or questions are holding you back?

How do you feel "led" by God in this season? How is God communicating with you and providing guidance? What helps you to be certain of His instructions?

Are you trusting God to heal your spiritual blind spots? Do you have the desire to see God more clearly, even if it means letting go of your preconceived notions of Him? Why or why not?

> Sometimes, we have trouble seeing the goodness of God because of our desire to do things our way.

Leaning into Hope

When my husband was young, he detested the taste of most medicines. These days, kids' medicines come in a variety of flavors, but at that time, the only flavor was blech. While most of us just took the medicine, made a sour face, and moved on, my husband bucked the system. His stubbornness was stronger than his desire to get better. One time when he was ill, his mom would bring his medicine and some water to his bedside, and he would wait for her to turn her back and then throw the uncoated pills over his head and behind his bed, tricking his mom into thinking he had taken them.

Well, by the grace of God, he got better without the pills. However, when they moved out of that house and the bed was pulled from the wall, the truth was exposed. His stubbornness, in the form of fifty little tablets strewn all over the floor, was there for all to see!

Sometimes, we have trouble seeing the goodness of God because our desire to do things our way, including coping mechanisms we've developed as a result of the wounds we've sustained in this broken world, disallows us from trusting God and seeing Him clearly. We can be so focused on our problems and our own strength, capability, or plan—the things we've fixed our sights on—that we fail to let God heal our spiritual vision so we can see Him and everything else more clearly. Sometimes healing can be a slow process. Yet we can be confident that God is patient and never stops working on our behalf.

Here's what we can take to the bank: God will be faithful to complete what He has started by continually asking us, "What do you see now?" and working to restore our vision until we are able to see clearly. We can trust God to heal our spiritual vision.

What do you see now—in other words, how is your spiritual vision? How do you see God, yourself, and others?

God:

Myself:

Others:

Ask God to reveal any spiritual blind spots or blurry vision—places in your life where you are not seeing with the eyes of Christ. What might be keeping you from seeing God, yourself, and others clearly right now?

How do you sense God inviting you to trust Him to heal your spiritual vision?

A Practical Next Step

What is one way Christ is inviting you to participate in the healing process so that your spiritual vision may be fully restored? Talk with God and journal your conversation.

Week 1 Wrap-up

I bought myself a gift recently. I decided I needed something in the Bermuda Triangle of seasons between my birthday in December, Valentine's Day in February, and Mother's Day in May. It wasn't an expensive purse or pair of shoes. I do not use a purse often, and my size 11 feet do not need one more reason to get calluses. No, I bought something that made me so happy.

I bought a bird feeder. Yep, I know. You are jealous of my gift-buying prowess, but hear me out. In a season of financial uncertainty, I needed a gentle reminder of the provision of God. I know with my mind that God provides for His people. One of His names is Jehovah Jireh—God Who provides. I know with my heart that He has always taken care of my family financially. But my eyes needed convincing.

My mom is totally into birds. She is the only person in my life who subscribes to the Audubon Society newsletters and takes great joy in discerning the call of each bird. In fact, years ago, we bought her an app that can help determine the type of bird and its call. I tried it once, my arms stretched as high as humanly possible so that the app could tell me which type of bird was nesting nearby, but I felt foolish. I looked like I was trying to be a human radio antenna. I am confident that it got the neighbors talking—and laughing.

When the feeder arrived, I removed it from its packaging—careful not to break the giant glass receptacle—filled it with seeds from the hardware store, and hung it outside our back door. For days, I would check for visitors to no avail. If there was a dinner bell for feathered friends, I would have rung it loudly.

Finally, two small birds arrived and perched themselves squarely on the feeder, enjoying the spoils therein. You would have thought that I created birds with the number of photos I took!

I can see the feeder from my living room. It serves as a wonderful reminder that if God values the birds of the air enough to feed them and the flowers in the field enough to dress them, then I need only trust Him.

Does that mean only happy things will happen to me? No, it means that no matter what befalls me, He loves me and will take care of me. Does that mean I have the guarantee to drive the nicest car? No. In fact, I drive an old (let's call it pre-vintage) vehicle these days, but that is no reflection on God's provision or protection. Does that mean I am promised to live in the nicest house on the block? Negative, Ghost Rider.

> The blessings of God are not measured strictly through the lens of material possessions, prestige, power, or popularity.

Some people talk a lot about "the blessings of God." Although this is not a bad thing, sometimes it can skew our perspective. The blessings of God are not measured strictly through the lens of material possessions, prestige, power, or popularity. Sometimes, the blessings of God look like grace when we have failed again. Or a crayon drawing from a neighbor kid when we have had an especially hard day. Or the next breath when loss and discouragement seem to belabor our breathing. Or a smile from a stranger when we feel like doing anything but smiling. Or a bird or two that come to feed when I need the reminder that God will indeed provide for me and my family, even when the financial forecast looks bleak.

This week we took a glance at a portion of the Sermon on the Mount where Jesus asks a question that truly gets to the heart of all our matters:

[25]"Therefore I tell you, do not worry about your life, what you will eat or drink; or about your body, what you will wear. Is not life more than food, and the body more than clothes? [26]Look at the birds of the air; they do not sow or reap or store away in barns, and yet your heavenly Father feeds them. Are you not much more valuable than they? [27]Can any one of you by worrying add a single hour to your life?

(Matthew 6:25-27)

When we read these verses out of context, it is easy to forget the things Jesus talks about earlier in Matthew 6. In verses 1-4, Jesus talks about giving to the needy. In verses 5-15, Jesus models and addresses prayer. In verses 6-18, Jesus uncovers the spiritual discipline of proper fasting. In verses 19-24, Jesus digs into the concept of treasures in heaven and on earth. And then, in verses 25-34, Jesus talks about worry regarding "stuff"—the provision of God and the futility of worry when God is involved. What a powerful progression of ideas: generosity, prayer, fasting, heaven-mindedness, and then the care of the Father. It feels like a love note from God written with the ink of the questions of Jesus asked in these verses on the stationery of our faith.

I love filling the feeder with seed and watching my new feathered friends hit the buffet with fervor. It has become a source of entertainment, for sure, but it also is a daily reminder that God loves His people. Not only is God familiar with our need; He asks us to "seek first His kingdom and His righteousness" (v. 33) so He can enjoy adding to us all the things we need.

This week we have examined the love, goodness, faithfulness, safety, and healing work of God through the lens of several questions of Jesus—all so we can know that God can be trusted. I hope that as these questions continue to speak to your heart and mind, they will help you to see God even more clearly and trust God more and more.

Of the questions we've explored, which one resonates most, and why?

What questions do you still have related to trusting God?

Read the week's memory verse, Psalm 28:7, slowly several times. Is there a word or phrase that catches your attention or touches your heart? What does God have to say to you about the word or phrase in light of your current life experience? How is God inviting you to respond?

Video Viewer Guide Week 1

Memory Verse: Psalm 28:7

Power:

The Lord is my _____.

Protection:

...and my _____

...and he _____ me.

Process:

...my heart _____ in him.

Praise:

My heart leaps for _____,

and with my song I _____ him.

Permission Slip:

This week we have examined God's love, goodness, faithfulness, safety, and healing work through questions Jesus posed—all so we can be assured that God can be trusted. As these questions continue to speak to both your heart and your mind, my prayer is that they will help you to see God and His trustworthy character even more clearly.

You have permission to have _____.

> Why, my soul, are you downcast?
> Why so disturbed within me?
> Put your hope in God,
> for I will yet praise him,
> my Savior and my God.
> (Psalm 42:5 NIV)

To awaken to the Spirit, we must awaken to _____.

How Can I Grow in My Faith?

MEMORY VERSE:

"Truly I tell you, if you have faith as small as a mustard seed, you can say to this mountain, 'Move from here to there,' and it will move. Nothing will be impossible for you."

(Matthew 17:20b)

When our kids were little, we would celebrate their birthdays by having them stand tall against one of the doorframes in our home and marking their gained height with their name and age. I remember leaning over their heads to mark their growth with accuracy and care. Now that our kids are fully grown (our daughter is 5'8" and our son is 6'5"), it is clear we know how to grow them tall in our house!

The truth is that their growth, though helped by good nutrition, is mostly based upon genetics. Wishing, hoping, and practicing height is not enough to ensure that tallness occurs.

This is similar to, yet different from, spiritual growth. God is the one who brings the growth in us, but we can position ourselves for growth and foster growth by cooperating with the work of God in us—and we can mark spiritual growth in our lives. This week, we are going to explore some of the questions of Jesus that lead us toward practical tools for fostering spiritual growth in cooperation with God: knowing Jesus, learning from the faith of others, remembering God's faithfulness in the past, praying, and living out our belief in Jesus.

If you feel like your spiritual growth is stunted, in a holding pattern, or just plain stagnant, you are not alone. Lots of people struggle with spiritual growth for various reasons, and even the most faithful of folks hit seasons when they feel like they are not growing, including folks in the Bible.

Peter was one of the apostles—the original twelve disciples (followers) of Jesus. He walked alongside Jesus for the three years of His ministry on earth. Peter saw Jesus heal and feed multitudes and resurrect people from the dead—undeniable miracles of God through Jesus—yet Peter's faith was imperfect.

When Jesus was arrested, Peter vacillated between fear and faith. He denied knowing Jesus, cursed, and fulfilled Jesus's prediction and prayer regarding Peter's faith failures (Mark 14:66-72; Luke 22:31-34).

Although we are not going to do a deep dive into the story of Peter this week, his story reminds us that we all are capable of faith inertia. Yet because of God's faithfulness, we're also capable of great growth despite any setbacks or challenges we might face in the spiritual journey!

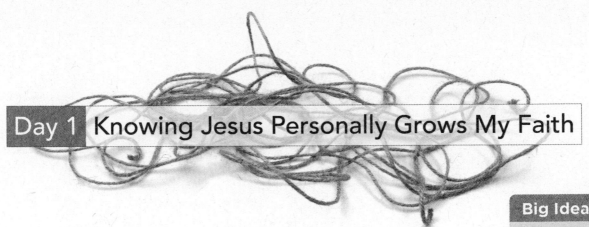

Day 1 Knowing Jesus Personally Grows My Faith

Big Idea

Jesus wants to help you know Him.

Jesus's Question:
"But what about you?" he asked.
"Who do you say I am?"
(Matthew 16:15)

The Question We Ask:
Who is Jesus to me?

Leaning into the Question

My memom, my maternal grandmother, was a class act. She was smart, interesting, capable, and beautiful, but more than that, she was a fierce cheerleader for her family. Although she and my pepaw (Texans give weird names to our grandparents, what can I say?) lived many states away, they always worked to know their grandkids well.

I wanted to be just like my memom. There were a few issues, however. I was taller than her by five inches by the time I was in fifth grade. She was smaller in frame and lower in volume than I have ever been. She had a sense of fashion that I can neither replicate nor afford.

She knew her way around their cattle ranch. She assisted cows in delivering calves, helped secure the perimeter fences like a boss, oversaw many employees, fought water moccasins, knew how to fish, and did it all with little perspiration or loss of temper.

Memom also believed in Jesus. Since faith was a bit foreign to me (we did not practice Christianity or any other religion in my immediate family), I was always intrigued by her Bible, her stories of Sunday school, and the hymns my pepaw would play on the organ in the living room.

Her faith was real; she lived with purpose, loved with fervor, served with passion, gave selflessly, and prayed consistently. So, it came as a great shock to those who knew her best that when her death was imminent, she began to have doubts. Like a cat being placed in a bathtub of water, she fought in the last days of her life, trying to avoid the inevitable and silence the doubts in her heart. But the questions kept invading her mind: *What if I was wrong all along and there is no heaven? What if this is all there is? If there is a heaven, why would God let me in? What if my sins are greater than God's capacity to forgive?*

Some might say her questions imply that her faith was not real. But I don't buy that. Anyone who has faith has had questions somewhere down the line, and my memom was no exception.

When you consider doubts you've had about God and faith, what stands out above the rest, and why?

Have you found resolution for any of your doubts? If so, what helped you? What doubts remain?

Have there been times in your life when God's provision, protection, or power turned your doubts into strengths of your faith? If so, explain briefly.

Leaning into the Scripture

I would say my memom's faith looked like Peter's. Peter had his share of doubts as well. This follower of Jesus was best known for his walk—or more accurately, drop—across the water. He had incredible faith in and fervor for Jesus, yet when he saw the wind and the waves, his faith was shaken (Matthew 14:30-32). Here are some other things we can surmise from the scriptures about Peter:

- He was a fisherman originally called Simon (Mark 3:16; Luke 6:14; John 1:42).
- He was married (Mark 1:30; 1 Corinthians 9:5).
- He had a mother-in-law whom Jesus healed (Mark 1:29-31; Luke 4:38-39).
- He was painfully aware of his shortcomings (Luke 5:8).
- He was often the spokesperson for the apostles (Matthew 15:15; 16:16; 18:21; 19:27; Mark 8:29; 10:28; Luke 9:20; 12:41; 18:28).

He also had grand moments of contradiction. After Peter confessed the identity of Jesus and was praised by Jesus for his faith and insight from the Holy Spirit, Jesus rebuked Peter for objecting to Jesus's predictions about His impending death (Matthew 16:23; Mark 8:33). He truly was a contradiction.

Aren't we all at times?

In Matthew 16, Jesus probes the opinions of His followers with three questions that spur their thinking and confession:

13When Jesus came to the region of Caesarea Philippi, he asked his disciples, "Who do people say the Son of Man is?"

14They replied, "Some say John the Baptist; others say Elijah; and still others, Jeremiah or one of the prophets."

*15"But what about you?" he asked. "**Who do you say I am?**"*

16Simon Peter answered, "You are the Messiah, the Son of the living God."
(Matthew 16:13-16, emphasis added)

Jesus was a masterful teacher, and one of His most powerful strategies was questions. As the Son of God, Jesus knew the answers to these questions. So why did He ask them? I cannot pretend to understand the mind of the Savior of the World; however, as a teacher, I can assume that His desire was to entice His followers into deeper thought and reflection.

Notice that the two questions in verse 15 are more pointed. Jesus wanted to get to the heart of the matter for them personally. And get to it, He did. His questions brought about a response from Peter, oft quoted in baptisms when talking about the identity of Jesus: "You are the Messiah, the Son of the living God."

But Jesus's question was not just for His apostles. It is for everyone. It is for you and me.

"What about you? Who do *you* say I am?" (emphasis added).

When did you first come to believe in God? Write the story briefly here:

How would you have answered Jesus's question—"Who do you say I am?"— at that time?

Leaning into Hope

I remember the first time I understood—as much as one can at ten years of age—who Jesus is. I did not know a single theologian's name. I could not tell you if I was pre-tribulation or post-tribulation, Calvinist or Arminian. I did not contemplate the Trinity, and I could not recite a scripture verse from memory (except maybe "Jesus wept"). But when I was challenged by a passionate preacher's sermon to contemplate the deity of Jesus, my confession was much like that of Peter: "He is God's Son!" I did not have all the answers, but I was confident that I knew the One who did.

Faith, however, is not only about salvation. It is a daily journey, an ongoing exercise in answering the question: "What about you? Who do you say I am?"

Perhaps to you Jesus is a skilled teacher. Or a great guy. Or a good example. Or your Savior, your only hope. The important thing for all of us is to keep learning about Jesus and getting to know Him so that our response to His question "Who do you say I am?" becomes passionate and personal.

Our thoughts, actions, behaviors, relationships, and our faith journey reflect our view of who we believe Jesus is. By asking ourselves this question about Jesus every day and giving it careful thought, prayer, and contemplation, we can uncover our honest views and doubts, share them with Jesus, and listen for His response. In this way, we can increase our fervor for God as we deepen our relationship with Jesus.

Friend, I know the journey of figuring out who Jesus is to you can be a difficult one. A confusing one. A frustrating one. But I can say from personal experience that it is one worth taking, indeed!

When Solomon was dropping truth bombs in Proverbs, this one was directed at his son but is perfect for us when we, too, are looking for wisdom in matters of faith—especially pertaining to Jesus:

> *My son, if you accept my words*
> *and store up my commands within you,*
> *²turning your ear to wisdom*
> *and applying your heart to understanding—*
> *³indeed, if you call out for insight*
> *and cry aloud for understanding*
> **⁴and if you look for it as for silver**
> **and search for it as for hidden treasure,**
> *⁵then you will understand the fear of the Lord*
> *and find the knowledge of God.*
> *⁶For the Lord gives wisdom.*
>
> (Proverbs 2:1-6a, emphasis added)

I have not been treasure-hunting with a map, pickax, and shovel lately, although bargain-hunting is most

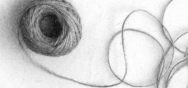

Faith is not only about salvation.

definitely a spiritual gift of mine. But here is the deal with trying to find hidden treasure, whether artifacts or a pair of jeans that fits perfectly or wisdom and understanding: it is hard. We spend a lot of time not finding anything, going down fruitless paths while wondering if the treasure might be there.

When we first seek to know God, it can feel much like this type of treasure hunt. It can involve quiet time without sensing God's presence, time in the Word without inspiration from God—definitely not a light from heaven or angels singing, as I've seen depicted on television!—or prayer without tangible proof that God hears us.

Some grow weary and miss the greatest treasure of all—a transformational relationship with the God who is the Creator of the Universe, the Savior of the World, the Holy Spirit who comes to live within us. All because they want the treasure without the seeking. They desire the valuables without learning where and how to search. They are not willing to put in the spiritual work—the spiritual disciplines or practices—to understand who Jesus is, what He did on the cross, and what He longs to do for and in each of us. And they are not willing to trust that in the process, *they* are the ones who will be found by the treasure Himself.

How about you? Are you willing to put in the spiritual work to come to know God, trusting that God is *seeking you*? The journey of faith requires us to answer Jesus's question—"Who do you say I am?"—not just once, when deciding to follow Him, but every day of our lives. And here's the good news: Jesus wants to help us know Him—to walk with us on the journey—so that we can answer the question passionately and personally every day of our lives!

What are five words or phrases you would use to describe Jesus?

What spiritual disciplines (practices) help you to seek and be found by God?

What is your favorite way to get to know Jesus better?

A Practical Next Step

Take your list of descriptors of Jesus (above) and write a paragraph explaining what you believe today about Jesus and why. Make it passionate and personal!

Day 2 The Faith of Others Grows My Faith

Big Idea

Faith doesn't have to be perfect to be real, and others can help us in our journey.

Jesus's Question:
"Where is your faith?" he asked his disciples.
(Luke 8:25)

The Question We Ask:
What if my faith wavers?

Leaning into the Question

I love heroes, don't you? I definitely have plenty of them.

I have incredible respect for gifted musicians. I dabble in music myself. I serve on my church's worship team, take voice lessons, can play limited scales on the piano, own a ukulele (notice I didn't say *play*), and can harmonize with almost anyone. But no one from the Rock & Roll Hall of Fame is calling me.

I have palpable esteem—and envy, if I'm honest—for professional athletes. I cry when a player wins Wimbledon or my Cowboys lose (I have done a *lot* of crying in some seasons), enjoy a volleyball game with the best of them, can consistently make a basket from the top of the key, and understand the rules of soccer. I played various sports through high school. But no one from the Baseball Hall of Fame is asking me to be a part of their museum.

I have a deep admiration for great orators. I teach written and verbal communications at two universities, speak at almost one hundred events a year, watch TED Talks on subjects I don't even care about, study the great speakers of our time, and practice my craft as much as possible. But no one from the White House is calling me to address the nation.

I could be discouraged. I could decide that if I can't be great, then there is no need to try. I could believe that if I waffle or waver then I'm disqualified. Instead, I find much comfort and encouragement in a collection of stories from the greats of another realm—the realm of faith.

Hebrews 11, often called the "Hall of Faith," recounts some of the greats in the Old Testament. I certainly am not as awesome as those mentioned in the chapter—heroes such as Noah, Abraham, Sarah, and many others. However, I must point out that none of them is included

because of musical talent, basketball prowess, or the ability to craft a strong introduction! (I couldn't resist!) No, it is their faith that put them there. All are men and women who, despite great challenges, displayed great faith. Their faith was great, yet as we will see, it was not perfect. I don't know about you, but that's an encouragement I need on the regular, because sometimes my faith wavers.

The chapter begins with this definition of faith: "confidence in what we hope for and assurance about what we do not see" (Hebrews 11:1). When I learned this verse as a teen, the version I memorized phrased the definition "the evidence of things not seen" (KJV).

Ask lawyers (or anyone like me who watches too many law dramas) about evidence, and they will tell you that evidence is collected, stored in a secure place, vital for getting to the truth, and often discovered after an investigator has asked a myriad of questions. When we read Hebrews 11, we find evidence *of* faith and *for* faith in the lives of biblical heroes.

> Now faith is confidence in what we hope for and assurance about what we do not see. ²This is what the ancients were commended for.
>
> ³By faith, we understand that the universe was formed at God's command, so that what is seen was not made out of what was visible.
>
> ⁴By faith Abel brought God a better offering than Cain did. By faith he was commended as righteous, when God spoke well of his offerings. And by faith, Abel still speaks, even though he is dead.
>
> (Hebrews 11:1-4)

Let me pause here for a moment. Notice how often the apostle Paul uses the pronoun "we" in this first paragraph. This chapter begins with us! Paul is including you and me, and the gazillions of Christians who have gone before us, to examine and collect evidence of the goodness and faithfulness of God through the faith of the men and women named here.

Paul's list of MVPs of faith begins with Abel. This son of Adam and Eve, a shepherd and seemingly good guy, offers an acceptable sacrifice to God and hacks off his brother in the process. Although there is no account in scripture of Abel doing something egregious, there also is no mention in scripture stating that Abel was perfect. Not one. Can imperfect people have genuine faith? Yes! Our background and track record cannot disqualify us from real faith.

Now, let's pick up where we left off.

⁵By faith Enoch was taken from this life, so that he did not experience death: "He could not be found, because God had taken him away." For before he was taken, he was commended as one who pleased God. ⁶And without faith it is impossible to please God, because anyone who comes to him must believe that he exists and that he rewards those who earnestly seek him.

(Hebrews 11:5-6)

> **Our mistakes cannot disqualify us from real faith.**

Enoch was also a super good guy, even though he named a child Methuselah. That kid had to endure junior high with that moniker—but I digress. Enoch was the great-great-great-great-grandson of Adam, who lived a crazy number of years—365, according to Genesis 5:23. We might say that he was pretty much the GOAT in faith—the greatest of all time because he lived so long. But if we read verses 22 and 24, we find a juicy detail about him. Though he lived 365 years, it says he walked faithfully with God for 300 years. That means there were 65 years that may have been less than stellar.

We *all* have lived years that were less than stellar—perhaps decades. But hear this good news: *our mistakes cannot disqualify us from real faith.*

Enoch's great-grandson, Noah, was also an upstanding citizen of faith, even if some of his neighbors thought him a bit weird.

> By faith Noah, when warned about things not yet seen, in holy fear built an ark to save his family. By his faith he condemned the world and became heir of the righteousness that is in keeping with faith.

(Hebrews 11:7)

Noah was not perfect (see Genesis 9:21), but the beauty is that despite his imperfections, God used him in mighty ways. More good news: *the perceptions of others cannot disqualify us from real faith.*

Notice that neither Noah's father, Lamech, nor his grandfather, Methuselah, is mentioned in this chapter on faith. Even more good news: *when our family background is not without issues, we can still collect evidence of the goodness of God.*

Now we come to Abraham.

> By faith Abraham, when called to go to a place he would later receive as his inheritance, obeyed and went, even though he did not know where he was going. ⁹By faith he made his home in the promised land like a stranger in a foreign country; he lived in tents, as did Isaac and Jacob, who were heirs with him of the same promise. ¹⁰For he was looking forward to the city with foundations, whose architect and builder is God. ¹¹And

by faith even Sarah, who was past childbearing age, was enabled to bear children because she considered him faithful who had made the promise.
[12]And so from this one man, and he as good as dead, came descendants as numerous as the stars in the sky and as countless as the sand on the seashore. . . .

[17]By faith Abraham, when God tested him, offered Isaac as a sacrifice. He who had embraced the promises was about to sacrifice his one and only son, [18]even though God had said to him, "It is through Isaac that your offspring will be reckoned." [19]Abraham reasoned that God could even raise the dead, and so in a manner of speaking he did receive Isaac back from death.

(Hebrews 11:8-12, 17-19)

I love me some Abraham! His life plays out like a three-season dramedy on Netflix. Unlike me, he seems to have been a morning person. Twice in Genesis we read that he got up "early the next morning" (Genesis 19:27; 22:3). One of those instances was when God asked him to sacrifice his son. I cannot get up early in the morning and make coffee without spilling some on the floor, so I cannot *imagine* making a choice with that kind of gravity at that hour. Abraham's faith was so strong, however, that he got up very early to obey God.

By that time, though, Abraham had been collecting evidence of God's goodness for a long time—sometimes with slipups on his end.

- Abraham left all he knew and traveled to a new land with his wife, Sarah (Genesis 12:1-5).
- Abraham tried to pass off Sarah as his sister (demonstrating a lack of faith in God's protection) (Genesis 20:2).
- Abraham took another wife at age eighty-five (demonstrating a lack of faith in God's promises) and became a father at eighty-six (Genesis 16).
- Abraham was visited by three strangers who reminded him of God's goodness, and at one hundred, he and Sarah became parents—despite their lack of faith in God's provision (Genesis 18; 21).

Abraham demonstrated faith and lack of faith, yet despite his spiritual waffling, God was patient as Abraham collected evidence of the goodness of God.

Hebrews 11 goes on to include the faith of Isaac, Jacob, Joseph, Moses's parents, Moses, the people of faith passing through the Red Sea, those at the battle of Jericho, Rahab (a prostitute), Gideon, Barak, Samson, Jephthah, David, Samuel, and the prophets. Take in this incredible news: *no culture, gender, hardship, persecution, social status, or occupation can disqualify us from real faith!*

Which of the faith heroes in Hebrews 11 stands out most to you, and why?

How are you encouraged by their imperfections, limitations, mistakes, and even spiritual waffling?

Leaning into the Scripture

With Hebrews 11 as our encouragement, let's look now to Jesus's question in Luke 8:

> ²²One day Jesus said to his disciples, "Let us go over to the other side of the lake." So they got into a boat and set out. ²³As they sailed, he fell asleep. A squall came down on the lake, so that the boat was being swamped, and they were in great danger.
>
> ²⁴The disciples went and woke him, saying, "Master, Master, we're going to drown!"
>
> He got up and rebuked the wind and the raging waters; the storm subsided, and all was calm. ²⁵"***Where is your faith?***" he asked his disciples.
>
> In fear and amazement they asked one another, "Who is this? He commands even the winds and the water, and they obey him."
>
> (Luke 8:22-25, emphasis added)

I can totally imagine this scene with Jesus and His posse. It looks like a road trip my family might take—except Jesus and the disciples are on the water, there are no incessant potty breaks, and there's probably a lack of the biblical equivalent of Cheez-It crackers.

Jesus was sleeping although He knew a storm was coming (He is God, after all). Even the seasoned fishermen on board were afraid. Andrew, Peter, James, and John were all fishermen by trade. When Jesus called them, Andrew and Peter were fishing, and James and John were mending nets with their father (Matthew 4:18-22). It is possible that Thomas, Nathaniel, and Philip also may have worked as fishermen, because all seven were fishing when Jesus appeared to them following His resurrection (John 21:2-8).

Jesus could sleep, no doubt, because He was well aware that His Father was in charge of the waves and could be trusted. But He asked His followers why they did not have the same confidence.

"Where is your faith?" he asked his disciples (Luke 8:25).

It is a question for all of us when the storms of life make us afraid. Do we trust? Are we confident in the faithfulness of God?

The beauty of this story, in my eyes, is that Jesus stilled the storms on the water and in the hearts of His followers, even when their faith was less than perfect. Even when their trust wavered, Jesus calmed their waves of uncertainty and fear.

When revisiting the great list of faith in Hebrews 11, many of those listed had a storm experience in their faith. Some showed greater trust than others, but even these MVPs of scripture had days when their imperfection coupled with the uncertainties of their circumstances rocked their spiritual boat. They remind us that faith doesn't have to be perfect to be real, and others can help us in our journey.

When have you faltered or wavered in faith? How did you find your footing again?

When has someone encouraged you to keep the faith when your faith was weak, as Jesus did the disciples? When have you been the one encouraging someone else?

Who are your "faith heroes," and how have they made a difference in your life?

A Practical Next Step

Call or visit with a friend or mentor and share where you are in your faith journey. Are you standing firm in faith or wavering and in need of some support and encouragement? Choose someone you trust who will listen without judgment or advice. If you feel comfortable, ask the person to pray with you.

Day 3 Remembering God's Faithfulness Grows My Faith

Big Idea

We can trust God without needing signs and wonders when we allow the evidence of God to focus our minds and hearts on God.

Jesus's Question:
"Why does this generation ask for a sign?"
(Mark 8:12)

The Question We Ask:
How can I have faith when times are hard?

Leaning into the Question

Yesterday we looked at part of Hebrews 11, but we stopped before the chapter got gnarly. After the long list of faith phenoms, we hit verse 35 where we read of people of faith who faced unimaginable hardships and persecution. When Starbucks is out of my iced tea mix, or I am stuck in traffic, or my lipstick melts in my car on a hot day, I feel tested; but in comparison to Hebrews 11:35-38, my ordinary problems are inconsequential.

35There were others who were tortured, refusing to be released so that they might gain an even better resurrection. 36Some faced jeers and flogging, and even chains and imprisonment. 37They were put to death by stoning; they were sawed in two; they were killed by the sword. They went about in sheepskins and goatskins, destitute, persecuted and mistreated—38the world was not worthy of them. They wandered in deserts and mountains, living in caves and in holes in the ground.
(Hebrews 11:35-38)

It seems like the evidence box for the goodness of God goes missing at verse 35. Where is God when all this bad stuff is happening to people who love Him?

Have you ever asked yourself that question? Perhaps a better question is this: when was the last time you asked yourself that question?

I spent much of my childhood at an amusement park called Santa Cruz Beach Boardwalk. As soon as I turned five, my dad took me on the largest roller coaster in the park, the Giant Dipper. At the time, five was considered "old enough" to ride. Height wasn't even a consideration. I am not sure who screamed more loudly, my dad or me, but it was a thrill I will never forget.

Roller coasters are such an amazing part of my life. On my wedding day, my dad gave me two roller-coaster tickets for the Big Dipper and wrote "for you and your new roller-coaster buddy" on the tag. He died just a few years later, but the sentiment of his note still rings true: my husband, Scott, and I continue to be roller-coaster buddies, and believe me, we have had more than our share of thrilling moments and ups and downs.

Because of our love for coasters, Scott and I have been part of the American Coaster Enthusiasts (ACE) club. Clubs can sound exclusive and prestigious, but believe me, this club is simply a bunch of fun, geeky thrill-ride nerds who like to ride coasters. Scott and I have ridden at least a hundred roller coasters together and have passed on our passion for thrill rides to our kids.

Because of my curiosity about coasters, I decided to learn about their history. In my research, I discovered that early roller coasters were not really all that great. They were thrilling, uncomfortable, and sometimes downright dangerous. In the sixteenth century, the Russians invented the ice slides—hills constructed of wood and ice. After climbing a massive set of stairs, courageous riders would position themselves on a block of ice with straw on top for cushioning and traverse down the slope. Even the French, the masterful creators of crème brûlée and crepes, could not cook up the perfect coaster. In the early 1800s, they created their own version, except it was wheeled.[1] The problem was that the wheels often fell off, leaving the riders battered and bruised.

My research then focused on the turn of the next century. At this time in roller-coaster history, inventors and businessmen partnered to create a new generation of thrill rides. The Coney Island *Rough Riders* roller coaster was infamous for its thrill and danger; before shutting down, it killed seven people in a five-year span, jumped the track, and catapulted sixteen people from their seats.[2] Its sister thrill ride *The Flip Flap Railway*, which was the first coaster with a circular loop, knocked riders unconscious and gave them whiplash due to its g-forces.[3]

So, the genesis of the modern roller coaster, with its continual ups and downs, was fraught with danger and even death. It's an apt metaphor for the often rocky and sometimes perilous journey of faith.

The followers of Jesus mentioned in Hebrews 11:35-38 must have felt like the riders of the first roller coasters at times—a continual series of ups and downs, often bringing danger or even death. We see this pattern of ups and down throughout the Gospels. Jesus's miraculous healings were highs; the fear that the religious leaders caused were lows. The feeding of thousands with just the contents of a lunchbox was a high. The death of Jesus was a devastating low. His resurrection on the third day was a high. You get the picture.

Despite the spiritual tumult, these faithful first-century church folk mentioned at the end of Hebrews 11 had been collecting the evidence of God's goodness and faithfulness through the accounts of Jesus, including the story of the boy who suffered with a seizure disorder:

> [14]*When they came to the crowd, a man approached Jesus and knelt before him.* [15]*"Lord, have mercy on my son," he said. "He has seizures and is suffering greatly. He often falls into the fire or into the water.* [16]*I brought him to your disciples, but they could not heal him."*
>
> [17]*"You unbelieving and perverse generation," Jesus replied, "how long shall I stay with you? How long shall I put up with you? Bring the boy here to me."* [18]*Jesus rebuked the demon, and it came out of the boy, and he was healed at that moment.*
>
> [19]*Then the disciples came to Jesus in private and asked, "Why couldn't we drive it out?"*
>
> [20]*He replied, "Because you have so little faith. Truly I tell you, if you have faith as small as a mustard seed, you can say to this mountain, 'Move from here to there,' and it will move. Nothing will be impossible for you."*
>
> (Matthew 17:14-20)

In the accounts of Jesus, sometimes it seems He is gently encouraging his followers to exercise their faith muscles, and sometimes it appears he is being stern. I wonder about the tone Jesus took here when he called them out for their lack of faith. Did he sound more like an exasperated or a patient parent, a frustrated or a persistent coach, an impatient or a diligent teacher?

The disciples had *seen* Jesus do amazing things, yet still they could not muster the faith necessary to help this young man.

As we saw yesterday, in Hebrews 11:1 faith is described as the "assurance about what we do not see." The disciples were firsthand witnesses to many miracles, yet

sometimes they struggled to exercise faith. So, if you sometimes have trouble believing God, especially in difficult circumstances—even when your evidence box of His faithfulness is full—you are not alone!

What are some of the amazing things you have seen God do?

How do you celebrate when you see God at work in your life?

How do you still struggle at times to exercise your faith muscles?

> If you sometimes have trouble believing God, especially in difficult circumstances, you are not alone!

Leaning into the Scripture

The disciples weren't the only ones who struggled to believe. Right after the account of Jesus feeding thousands with a few fish and some bread, we discover that some of the religious leaders were up to something:

> *[11]The Pharisees came and began to question Jesus. To test him, they asked him for a sign from heaven. [12]He sighed deeply and said, "**Why does this generation ask for a sign?** Truly I tell you, no sign will be given to it." [13]Then he left them, got back into the boat and crossed to the other side.*
>
> (Mark 8:11-13, emphasis added)

The Pharisees were religious scholars; they knew the scriptures we call the Old Testament and the God described therein. But they did not understand that Jesus was the manifestation of those scriptures (John 1:1-4) and the Son of God. They wanted evidence and asked Jesus for a sign to prove who He is—even though the evidence was in all Jesus had already done.

I love that John notes in verse 12 that Jesus "sighed deeply." My kids know that when I sigh, it usually means I am either tired or tired of their shenanigans, or both. When I sigh deeply, they realize that they need to bring coffee and prepare to be grounded for a year (just kidding—well, not about the coffee part).

The Pharisees wanted their evidence box to be filled with miraculous signs and wonders, but if they had reviewed their biblical history of Moses, they would have remembered that signs and wonders alone are not enough to prove anything. Moses did many signs and wonders (Deuteronomy 34:11; Acts 7:36)—all to point to the power and majesty of God—yet Pharaoh did not believe.

Jesus was exasperated with the Pharisees because instead of looking to God, they were looking to signs. They were doing what many of us do, putting their trust in signs and miracles instead of in the giver of those signs and miracles: the ultimate Source of truth. God is the ultimate source of truth and deserves our reverence and trust, but like the Pharisees, we can sometimes make an idol out of the evidence instead of allowing it to point us to the Source.

Here are some examples of the evidence of God's goodness and trustworthiness—all pointing us to the Source:

- The sun came up today.
- There is air in your lungs.
- The cells in your body are working together to allow your eyes to read this page, process the information, and agree or disagree with its contents.
- A baby's laughter.
- The taste of freshly baked bread (sorry to all my gluten-free friends).
- The Grand Canyon.
- Hawaii—or any other beautiful place.
- Hugh Jackman (OK, maybe that is just my perspective, but I can tell you that I marvel at God's work when I look at the actor).

But it is idolatry if I look to any of these things for strength, guidance, wisdom, or comfort, and it makes the evidence, instead of the Source, the object of my trust. I believe this is the message for us at the heart of Jesus's question. We can trust God without needing signs and wonders when we allow the evidence of God's faithfulness to focus our minds and hearts on God.

Leaning into Hope

Sometimes God displays His goodness and power through dramatic and miraculous signs and wonders, and it is easy to fill our evidence box when those things happen. But oftentimes God works miracles in the mundane, under the radar of our consciousness. So, how do we heighten our awareness and choose to see the amazing in the ordinary events of life? How can we allow the evidence of God's faithfulness to deepen our trust in God?

In my experience, noticing and giving thanks for the evidence of God's faithfulness is a practice like any other healthy habit. Here are a few ideas:

- Regularly choose to list things for which you are thankful (that God created or put into place), especially when life feels defeating or bleak.
- Look to the lives of others. Sometimes just being a witness to the faithfulness of God in the everyday lives of others can bolster our faith. Other times, we can ask others to testify about the work of God in their lives.
- Look to the lives of those in scripture. As we've seen, Hebrews 11, the great hall of faith, is filled with stories of God's faithfulness in the lives of the patriarchs and matriarchs of the faith. And there are countless stories of God's faithfulness throughout the Scriptures. When difficulties come, their stories can serve to fill our evidence box and act as a map for navigating the rough terrain of life.
- Remind yourself of God's faithfulness by opening your evidence box to others. When someone else's ride of faith is rocky or perilous, you can extend a hand of encouragement by sharing your stories of God's faithfulness in the rough seasons of your journey.

Even if we do not see signs and wonders, we can find hope in noticing the ordinary ways God shows Himself faithful every day. These everyday "signs" serve as evidence that focuses our minds and hearts on God, deepening our love and increasing our trust.

Name some things in your "evidence box" for God's goodness and faithfulness gathered this week:

What helps you to believe when you do not see?

How do your actions or behaviors speak of—give evidence of—your faith?

Do you have a "roller-coaster buddy" in your life to share the highs and lows of your faith journey? If so, how does this buddy encourage you to have faith? If not, who is someone in your life who might become this kind of faith friend?

A Practical Next Step

Make a time line of your life, adding major life events. Are there more ups than downs? More downs than ups? Below your time line, list some of the evidence of God's goodness and faithfulness to you in all of these circumstances. Then take a few moments to express your thanks to God.

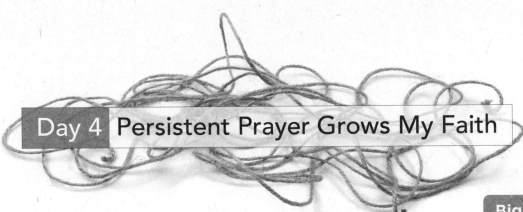

Day 4 Persistent Prayer Grows My Faith

Jesus's Question:
*"However, when the Son of Man comes,
will he find faith on the earth?"*
(Luke 18:8)

The Question We Ask:
Why should I keep praying?

Leaning into the Question

Though the mountain town where we live is a mile high in elevation, we are not often blessed with snow. When it does snow, however, it parallels the Hallmark Channel—it is pretty, shallow, and short-lived. I am not sure I would love it as much if it was a constant companion, decimated work schedules, and resulted in my car being pocked with ice melt chemicals, but I really love it.

One winter day, we got more than the usual amount of snow. The town looked like a snow globe—every surface was covered with a powdery pancho, and the sky continued to deliver a steady dose of frozen precipitation. I especially love snow when I am inside, with the fire blazing in the fireplace and my family safely by my side. The evening of this great snow, however, my idyllic snow scenario had a hiccup. Our elder child had a shift at work. She often closes at the restaurant where she is employed, which means she leaves the establishment well after her parents have gone to bed.

Though it had been snowing most of the afternoon, I was confident she could safely make it home. Why? Because the evidence was stacked in her favor.

- **Reliability.** She has driven in the snow many times before. She is a careful driver—I know because I have ridden as a passenger in her vehicle many times. I have been collecting evidence of her reliability since she got her license.
- **Reality.** Her car was in working order, and the streets were clearish—at least when I headed to bed. Her work was less than two miles from the safety of her warm bed. The snow had not stuck to the streets yet, and I knew she would call us if she felt unable to maneuver in the weather.

- **Relationship.** Our daughter is level-headed, reasonable, and responsible. She is not perfect, but no one short of Jesus is. I trust her because I know her well and trust her character.

In our family, if someone is away from home after the rest of us have gone to bed, we leave the hall light on. If the light is turned off, it is a signal for this mama that everyone is safe. So, the morning after it started snowing, I was relieved to wake up and see that, despite our getting almost eight inches of snow overnight, the light was off, which meant our daughter was home.

Why do I tell you this? Because whenever I am facing a faith-testing situation and I am tempted to give up on prayer, I go through this same filtering process of the three *R*s with God.

- When my dad got cancer, how did I know God could be trusted?
- When he succumbed to his illness and died, how could I be certain that God would work it for good?
- When my husband and I could not seem to get pregnant, how did I know that God would provide for our emotional needs?
- When I lost my job, how did I know that God would provide manna and encouragement?

Because of the three *R*s!

Reliability. God has a long track record. His rap sheet of loving deeds, faithful provision, miraculous works, and extensions of grace is not limited to the chronicles in the Bible; it includes all the faithful acts He has done in my life and yours—all the eventual answers to prayer, though not always in the ways we expect. Do my stories always get the fairytale ending I want? Hardly, but God continues to affirm His reliability as the One who works in my best interests—for my good and the good of His people. Always. My evidence box is full.

Reality. The reality is that I am better off trusting my plans and concerns to God than trying to do things on my own. I can hardly draw stick figures, so I certainly should not trust the artistry of my life to my own pencil. The reality is that although I am a capable person, God has proven again and again to be more capable in every area of my life. He knows all, sees all, is not limited to time or space, loves me like crazy, and is always good.

Relationship. This is the big one. What allows me to persist in prayer and eventually relinquish control to God—though not always without wailing and gnashing of teeth, tears, and a few unsuccessful attempts—is our relationship. I trust Him because I know Him and His character. Trustworthy is who He is. His nametag at

mixers could read "Hello, my name is TRUST ME." Why? Because we are His and He loves us. That doesn't make things easy, but it does make even the hard things manageable because we are never alone or forgotten. God hears our prayers and is for us.

When was the last time you could easily identify God's work in your life? Describe it briefly.

Which of the three *R*s is easiest for you when it comes to trusting God and His goodness?

Which of the three *R*s is most difficult for you when it comes to trusting God and His goodness?

Leaning into the Scripture

At the beginning of Luke 18, Jesus shares a parable with His apostles. He is talking specifically about prayer, but He ends the parable with a poignant question—for them and for us:

> Then Jesus told his disciples a parable to show them that they should always pray and not give up. ²He said: "In a certain town there was a judge who neither feared God nor cared what people thought. ³And there was a widow in that town who kept coming to him with the plea, 'Grant me justice against my adversary.'
>
> ⁴"For some time he refused. But finally he said to himself, 'Even though I don't fear God or care what people think, ⁵yet because this widow keeps bothering me, I will see that she gets justice, so that she won't eventually come and attack me!'"
>
> ⁶And the Lord said, "Listen to what the unjust judge says. ⁷And will not God bring about justice for his chosen ones, who cry out to him day and night? Will he keep putting them off? ⁸I tell you, he will see that they get

justice, and quickly. **However, when the Son of Man comes, will he find faith on the earth?**"

(Luke 18:1-8, emphasis added)

Jesus reminds those closest to Him—which now includes you and me—of the importance of prayer in our lives of faith. We can see the 3 *R*s in the story.

Reliability. God is the Righteous Judge. In this story, we are introduced to a judge who is neither just nor caring. In contrast, God both loves us and works in our best interest. He desires to hear the cries of our hearts and our pleas for justice.

Reality. Few are fervent in prayer, but God hears the prayers of His people and responds. He does not put us off but is always working to bring justice and do His good work in our lives. Even when we do not get the answer we are hoping for, God always hears our prayers and our desires and benevolently works to shape us more into the likeness of His Son.

Relationship. God loves us and wants to be good to us. Our relationship with God is secure not because of how good we are but because of how good He is. We cannot win His affections with our good deeds, although many of us try; He simply loves us because we are His. As our heavenly Father, He desires to bless and keep us in His care as well as have a healthy relationship with us.

> **How does Jesus's story of the righteous judge help you to see the reliability of God, the reality of God's goodness and faithfulness, and the relationship God desires with us? What new insights does it give you?**

> **Think of an area where your faith is being tested. How can you apply the 3 *R*s—reliability, reality, and relationship—to strengthen your faith and help you persist in prayer?**

Leaning into Hope

When I hear a screaming toddler throwing a tantrum at the local Target, I praise God that my children are grown (just being honest). When my kids were young and a tantrum occurred, my prayer was not that they would get what they wanted but that they would quickly grow out of that very loud and annoying season.

God desires that we grow in our faith even when—and perhaps especially when—we don't get what we want.

> God desires that we grow in our faith even when— and perhaps especially when—we don't get what we want.

For years, I perceived prayer to be fancy words used to cajole God into doing what I wanted or nagging Him into acquiescing to my desires. As I've grown in Christ, I've come to recognize that prayer is truly a gift to me. Prayer is access to the God of the Universe as well as an opportunity for Him to bolster my faith through His goodness. Those who consistently and persistently pray and seek the face of God grow in patience and faith.

Prayer builds our faith as we wait and come to trust God to answer. Prayer is not about the number of times we pray, how long we pray, or the fancy words we use when we pray; it's about our growing faith in the One who answers prayer. Prayer helps us to grow a confident faith, knowing that God is for us and can be trusted even though He may not answer our prayers in the way we want Him to. Persistent prayer shifts our focus from *what* we desire and *when* we want an answer to *who* God is and the persons He is growing us into. It brings us to a place of surrender where we desire God's plans and purposes over our own. It deepens our relationship and enables us to love God even more.

Wherever you find yourself today, my friend, be encouraged that persisting in prayer, while trusting in the character of God, *will* increase your faith!

How has your perspective on prayer changed over the years?

How has prayer changed you?

Do you have a plan or format you follow to consistently seek God's face in prayer?

A Practical Next Step

God is at least as good as a righteous judge and as loving as a caring parent—and infinitely more so! Rather than praying the same prayer over and over like a broken record, try the Quaker practice called "holding in the light." Picture the person(s) you are praying for—or those involved in the situation you are praying for—in your mind. Then picture them surrounded and covered by the glory of God's presence—God's healing light. "Hold" them in prayer in this way without words, trusting that the Holy Spirit who intercedes for us with groanings too deep for words is doing the praying.

Day 5 | Believing Jesus Grows My Faith

Big Idea

Believing Jesus empowers us to put our faith into action.

Jesus's Question:
*"Don't you believe that I am in the Father,
and that the Father is in me?"*
(John 14:10)

The Question We Ask:
Do I really believe Jesus is who He says He is?

Leaning into the Question

Thrift shopping is not just a pastime for me; it is part adventure, part hunting expedition, and part spiritual gift. I love finding bargains, uncovering treasures, and exploring others' castoffs. I feel that many of these items have a story to tell and I'm obligated to tell it.

I came by this love of thrifting honestly. My grandparents resold collectibles in their retirement years. My grandmother taught me young to spot Depression glass and valuable pottery of old. Oftentimes when I was at a garage sale and said I wanted to buy something for my grandmother, the person would give it to me for almost nothing. No one knew that my grandmother would turn around and sell it for a pretty penny. Looking back, it may have lacked integrity, but I just thought it was fun.

The secret is knowing enough about each item's history and value to discern if you've found a true treasure. It takes research, practice, and a lot of hours of rummaging through "stuff." As far as I know, I've never found something in my treasure-hunting of significant value.

Recently, a rare bowl from fifteenth-century China was sold at a yard sale in Connecticut. The bowl, which later was auctioned off for over $700,000, was purchased at the yard sale for only $35 by an antiques enthusiast. The enthusiast had done extensive research, had seen various Ming Dynasty artifacts, and had a feeling this piece was something spectacular. The treasure hunter emailed Sotheby's—one of the world's largest brokers of fine art, jewelry, and collectibles—for an evaluation after bringing the piece home.

Only after careful in-person inspection by trained specialists did Sotheby's confirm that the bowl was from the 1400s. The bowl's smoothness, silky glaze, and floral designs are all indicative

of that period, as is its shape—like that of a lotus flower. So, the inkling of the yard sale buyer was supported by a team of researchers from the auction house.

Angela McAteer, the head of Sotheby's Chinese Works of Art Department, said of the piece, "This exceptionally rare floral bowl, dating to the 15th century, epitomizes the incredible, once in a lifetime discovery stories that we dream about as specialists in the Chinese Art field."[4]

As far as scientists and collectors are concerned, there are only seven such bowls in the world. The other six are in museums around the world. How this particular bowl ended up in Connecticut is a mystery, but the story of this find makes me even hungrier to head to the nearest estate sale. There's something compelling about finding a treasure—the genuine article. And this is certainly true regarding our faith in Jesus as well.

Our faith in Jesus, the most precious commodity we can ever possess, is measured differently from the precious collectible discussed above. The bowl was old, but long-standing faith in Jesus does not necessarily mean it is more valuable. The antique was hidden, but faith that is hidden makes it less valuable to a world that needs to hear about the love of Jesus. The bowl was considered a once-in-a-lifetime discovery, but faith in Jesus is valuable because it is readily available to all who believe in Christ as Lord.

> Faith in Jesus is valuable because it is readily available to all who believe in Christ as Lord.

Leaning into the Scripture

In John 14, there is a beautiful conversation between Jesus and two of his disciples, one much more valuable than a pricey antique. Though we looked at this exchange on Week 1, Day 4 of our study, we focused then on a different question of Jesus: *don't you know me?*

Today our gaze is fixed on verse 10, where we find another question that sharpens our focus even more on the genuine article of faith, the real treasure. Let's revisit the conversation again:

> [5]*Thomas said to him, "Lord, we don't know where you are going, so how can we know the way?"*

> [6]*Jesus answered, "I am the way and the truth and the life. No one comes to the Father except through me. [7]If you really know me, you will know my Father as well. From now on, you do know him and have seen him."*

> [8]*Philip said, "Lord, show us the Father and that will be enough for us."*

> [9]*Jesus answered: "Don't you know me, Philip, even after I have been among you such a long time? Anyone who has seen me has seen the Father. How can you say, 'Show us the Father'? [10]****Don't you believe that I am in the Father, and that the Father is in me?*** *The words I say to you*

I do not speak on my own authority. Rather, it is the Father, living in me, who is doing his work. [11]Believe me when I say that I am in the Father and the Father is in me; or at least believe on the evidence of the works themselves. [12]Very truly I tell you, whoever believes in me will do the works I have been doing, and they will do even greater things than these, because I am going to the Father. [13]And I will do whatever you ask in my name, so that the Father may be glorified in the Son. [14]You may ask me for anything in my name, and I will do it."

(John 14:5-14, emphasis added)

Jesus asks Philip, "Don't you believe that I am in the Father, and that the Father is in me?" With this question, Jesus is saying that He and the Father are one. Jesus is God with us. He Himself is the genuine article, the great treasure.

If the bowl had stayed in the attic of some old house forever, its value never would have been discovered. Similarly, if we do not put our faith in who Jesus is—God with us—into practice, the strength and value of our faith will never be fully realized.

Perhaps sometimes our faith wavers not because there is no evidence that God can be trusted but because we have not put our faith in Jesus into practice—we have not fully believed who He is and therefore chosen to do the "works" He did; and as a result, we have not experienced the active faith to which He calls us. Of course, our salvation is not based on our works, but the works that come after salvation as we serve the Lord can serve as a bellows to the fire of our faith, igniting the world.

We discovered in Hebrews 11 that our faith cannot be negated by background, choices, others' perceptions, gender, culture, hardship, persecution, social status, occupation, or the ups and downs of life—although those things can profoundly affect it. Rather, our faith is between us and the One who fearfully and wonderfully made us to do good works: "For we are God's handiwork, created in Christ Jesus to do good works, which God prepared in advance for us to do" (Ephesians 2:10). Our faith rests on what we believe to be true about Jesus, and the test of this is our actions—our good works.

Obviously, good works look different for each person, but for someone who embraces her responsibility as the "handiwork" (some translations use "workmanship") of God, good works are a natural by-product of relationship with God. God takes our experiences, training, history, skill sets, and passions and uses them for the good of the world and His glory. Handiwork, or workmanship, is doing epic work such as feeding the homeless, sheltering the disenfranchised, loving the unlovable, fighting for justice, and winning others to Christ. Equally important yet less flashy, workmanship

is serving in children's ministry, taking out the trash, wiping behinds in the nursery, making cookies for a lonely neighbor, or hosting a Bible study. There is no set task list for those in Christ, but there is a definite call on each of us to live as the handiwork of God, doing the works of Jesus.

> **How do your actions communicate your faith in who Jesus is? How are you putting your faith into practice by doing the works of Jesus?**

Leaning into Hope

As a family, we journeyed through a curriculum on world view years ago. It is an amazing journey through logic and faith, and we have enjoyed grappling with some pretty big issues together as a result. One of the most compelling and convicting questions the facilitator asked is "Do you *really* believe what you really believe?"

What a silly question, right?

In the comfort of our chairs, when he posed the question, I thought, *Of course, I really believe.* But in the discomfort of heartbreak, disappointment, betrayal, loss, grief, anger, and frustration, I have to ask myself: Do I *really* believe that God can be trusted? Do I have faith that is not just a collection of evidence but active and sure? Do you?

> **Answer as honestly as you possibly can: do you really believe what you really believe [about Jesus]?**

> **How does the discomfort of heartbreak, disappointment, betrayal, loss, grief, anger, and frustration affect your faith?**

By the way, for those of you who are especially discerning, you and I did cover one of the verses from this section of scripture in week 1, but I wanted us to focus on another question Jesus posed and bring out new encouragement for us both.

Jesus asked Philip and the others listening, "Don't you believe that I am in the Father, and that the Father is in me? (John 14:10). When He asked if they believed that He and God are connected, are one, it must have sounded almost scandalous. But to us, to those who know that Jesus is Immanuel, God with us, who conquered sin and death and died for our sins, the question is: do we *really* believe it? If we really believe that Jesus is who He said He is—God with us and now, through the Holy Spirit, God within us—it will change our behaviors, our thoughts, our goals, and our lives. Believing Jesus empowers us to do the works of Jesus in this world and put our faith into action.

Describe a time when you have actively lived out your faith in Jesus, Immanuel—God with us and now within us.

Describe a time when your faith in Jesus as Immanuel, God with us and now within us, was lacking—when you did not have faith to do the works of Jesus.

What might help bolster your faith in Jesus, Immanuel, and help you put your faith into action in the world?

A Practical Next Step

Read Psalm 77:11-12 in the translation of your choice.
The Message translation is as follows:

Once again I'll go over what God has done,
lay out on the table the ancient wonders;
I'll ponder all the things you've accomplished,
and give a long, loving look at your acts.

Compare the two translations. What is the psalmist urging us to do? Now consider that Jesus is the culminating treasure of all God's works and wonders. How might you ponder who Jesus is and take a loving look at what He has done?

Week 2 | Wrap-up

I was in my early twenties when I lost my dad to cancer, and I did not deal well with the emotional aftermath. I would be fine for a day or two and then something would trigger me: a song on the radio, a child with his or her father in the grocery store, or a smell that reminded me of him, and the tears would well up in my eyes. I had a pit in my stomach that lasted for months. One day I realized it was time to reach out for some support.

Fortunately for me, my husband was serving at a church that had a counselor on staff. She was a bright and engaging woman who had a genuine concern for others, and I knew I could trust her. Our first counseling session was mostly just connecting, getting to know each other better. It was surface, superficial, and pleasant.

But the sessions that followed got progressively harder. She began to ask more questions about my childhood and the relationship I had with my dad. I love my dad. I think he did his absolute best to love my sister and me, but like all of us, he was imperfect. So, his best was still broken. His parents loved him imperfectly, and when one puts the abuse of alcohol in the mix, the broken can become even greater.

But I did not want to talk about my past. I was struggling in the present. I was wanting to subside the flood of emotions that seemed to come with no rhyme or reason. I wanted to heal from the loss. But she kept asking about the past. Exasperated with one of her questions, I asked, "Can we just focus on right now? My struggle is right now."

She lovingly and patiently looked at me. We sat in silence for a moment. "Our past experiences are the stones on the path to our present. I can't help you get where you want to go without understanding the path."

This week, we explored questions of Jesus as they pertain to our faith. Much like the past experiences that serve as stones on the path to the present, the experiences we have with God serve as stones on the path of our faith.

With each experience, both good and bad, our faith is shaped, bolstered, reshaped, and strengthened. When we couple our faith (Week 2) with the character of God (Week 1), we can walk a path of freedom, hope, and joy knowing that God has our backs (and our fronts!).

Of the questions we've explored, which one resonates most, and why?

> The experiences we have with God serve as stones on the path of our faith.

What questions do you still have about growing in faith?

Read the week's memory verse, Matthew 17:20b, slowly several times. Is there a word or phrase that catches your attention or touches your heart? What does God have to say to you about the word or phrase in light of your current life experience? How is God inviting you to respond?

Video Viewer Guide Week 2

How Can I Grow in My Faith?

Memory Verse

Matthew 17:20b NIV

Affirmation:

"Truly I _____ you…"

Stipulation:

"…if you have faith as small as a _____ _____"

Relocation:

"…you can say to this mountain, 'Move from here to there,' and it _____ _____."

Proclamation:

"_____ will be impossible for you."

Permission Slip:

This week, we unpack some really big ideas like Jesus wants to help you know Him; faith doesn't have to be perfect to be real and others can help us in our journey; we can trust God without needing signs and wonders when we allow the evidence of God to focus our minds and hearts on God; persisting in prayer, while trusting in the character of God, increases our faith; and finally, believing Jesus empowers us to put our faith into action.

You have permission not to _____ _____ _____.

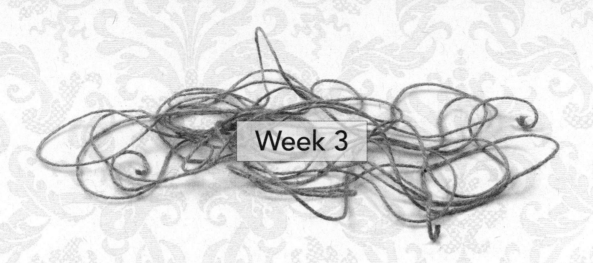

Why Should I Pray?

MEMORY VERSE:

This is the confidence we have in approaching God: that if we ask anything according to his will, he hears us.

(1 John 5:14)

Recently, our daughter, Judah, got in a car and moved across the country to pursue her dream of performing. I miss having her in our house so much, but I am so thankful for the ability to stay in touch via text, telephone, various apps, and sometimes even handwritten letters. These tools allow me to hear her heart and understand her more clearly.

Prayer is a way to stay in touch with God—with His heart, His voice, His will.

But prayer can often be underused, underappreciated, and underexplored. Even though it is an all-access pass to communicate with the God of the Universe, sometimes busyness, pride, uncertainty, and laziness stop us from using this "pass."

Our memory verse this week, 1 John 5:14, when taken out of context, can be misunderstood to mean that we pray only to get what we want. But prayer is about knowing God more, being confident in Him alone, and realizing that He hears us when we ask for things that coincide with His best for us.

If you struggle with prayer—whether it's finding a consistent time to pray or listening when God speaks or being unsure of what you hear from God—you are not alone, friend. We all have days when our prayer life is languid, or we have trouble hearing God, or we question what we have heard after God does answer.

This is not a new problem. In the Scriptures we see many examples of people who struggled with hearing and trusting God in prayer, including Abraham, the patriarch of our faith. You may know that God promised Abraham a child, but did you know God talked with Abraham not once but multiple times about having a son and descendants (see Genesis 12:7; 13:14-17; 15:4-6, 18; 17:1-8, 15-16)? I don't know about you, but I can relate to needing God to repeat Himself!

This week we will explore some of the many facets of prayer: intimate communication with God, learning to listen and look for God, God's goodness, our desires in prayer, and choosing God's best in prayer. Understanding these aspects of prayer will help us to hear God's heart and understand Him more clearly.

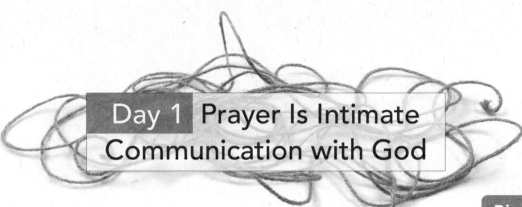

Day 1 Prayer Is Intimate Communication with God

Jesus's Question:
"What do you want me to do for you?"
(Matthew 20:32)

The Question We Ask:
Can I trust Jesus with my needs and desires?

Big Idea

Prayer is a relationship in which you feel safe to communicate what you desire.

Leaning into the Question

The Olympic Games are a highlight in our house. My husband is not a huge fan of sports, but when the Olympics are on, we wear red, white, and blue daily; operate on little sleep; and enjoy hours of coverage, savoring every personal interest story, ancillary interview, and awards ceremony. It is great when athletes from the United States win, but we think the Olympics are about humans from all countries doing the unimaginable and achieving things beyond their perceived capabilities. For us as spectators, it is all about the process, not really the winning.

But for many of the athletes and the countries they represent, it is all about winning. Some athletes have trained since they slept in a crib and have given up going to traditional schools, living with their families, having regular social lives, and eating junk food—all to win. They define success by medal counts, not by process. They go to the Olympics to win.

Much like winning, prayer is a tricky thing—not because it is complicated but because it is so personal. As a result, we define it and understand it differently.

At the core, prayer is communication—communication with a Higher Power. But it also is recognizing our need for help, our incapability to accomplish things on our own. It is humility tangled with hope.

When humility and hope intertwine, and our hearts are focused on the One who answers prayer, our thoughts and desires begin to align more with His.

For some, the greatest question is not how to pray but why. Does God hear our prayers? Can prayer change God's mind? Is prayer more about how it changes us or how it changes the circumstances about which we are praying?

What other questions do you have about prayer?

How do you recognize when God is at work in your life answering prayer? If it is not the answer you are looking for, what might it look like for you to lean into your belief in Jesus and your loving relationship with Him?

Every so often, I get tired of extra clutter in our house. We accumulate so much "stuff" that not everything has its own place, and I suddenly get a wild hair to throw everything in a box and drive directly to the closest thrift store to donate it.

I have been known to donate things that do not belong to me. My family has heard me say at least a gazillion times, may I add, that if something is important, it should be put away. If my kids leave items on the kitchen counter or the living room floor too long, after a few warnings, I will collect the treasures, wait a week to see if the owner "misses" them, and then give them away to my favorite nonprofit organization.

Some people get buyer's remorse, but I have the opposite issue. Sometimes I get giver's remorse. Sometimes, after I drop a box off for donation, I get a creeping suspicion that I have made a huge mistake. A giant mistake. A colossal mistake.

I certainly don't own much of great value. I do not own a single Ming vase, Fabergé egg, or pair of Jimmy Choo shoes, but I do like my stuff. I think we all do. Still, occasionally I donate something that I regret later.

I think most of us can relate to *really* wanting something, getting said something, and then losing interest in it. Thrift stores are filled with people's old castoffs that were once prized possessions.

Sometimes, I have a thrift-store mentality regarding answers to my prayers. There have been times when I *really* wanted something I did not think possible but I actually got it, and although I praised God in the moment, the luster of it dimmed in my mind. At times it is only after reviewing my prayer journal that I even remember the amazing ways God has answered some of my prayers.

How long after we receive what we pray for do we forget to be thankful?

Leaning into the Scripture

In Matthew 20, we meet two blind men who really want something—the gift of sight:

> ²⁹*As Jesus and his disciples were leaving Jericho, a large crowd followed him.* ³⁰*Two blind men were sitting by the roadside, and when they heard that Jesus was going by, they shouted, "Lord, Son of David, have mercy on us!"*
>
> ³¹*The crowd rebuked them and told them to be quiet, but they shouted all the louder, "Lord, Son of David, have mercy on us!"*
>
> ³²*Jesus stopped and called them. "What do you want me to do for you?" he asked.*
>
> ³³*"Lord," they answered, "we want our sight."*
>
> ³⁴*Jesus had compassion on them and touched their eyes. Immediately they received their sight and followed him.*
>
> (Matthew 20:29-34)

Jesus asks this same question—"What do you want me to do for you?"—two other times (Mark 10:51; Luke 18:41); and two of these three times, He is talking to a person afflicted with blindness. Jesus's questions seem almost superfluous. Everyone can "see" what these folks are asking for: they ask for mercy, but what they want is sight.

So, why does Jesus ask them what they want from Him? Why would He ask when it is so obvious?

Jesus, in my opinion, was wanting the men to articulate the true cry of their hearts—to communicate the one thing they *really* desire. He certainly knows their desires, but there is value in having them admit their need and state their hope.

If God already knows our hearts and the desires therein, why must we pray?

Well, God's Word has much to say on the subject. First Timothy 2 starts with the following charge to believers about worship: "I urge, then, first of all, that petitions, prayers, intercession and thanksgiving be made for all people" (v. 1).

We ask God because He instructs us to. The process of admitting our need and asking for help from God is His desire for us.

Song of Songs also provides insight for why we should pray:

> *Place me like a seal over your heart,*
>   *like a seal on your arm;*
> *for love is as strong as death,*
>   *its jealousy unyielding as the grave.*
> *It burns like blazing fire,*
>   *like a mighty flame.*
>
> *Many waters cannot quench love;*
>   *rivers cannot sweep it away.*
> *If one were to give*
>   *all the wealth of one's house*
>   *for love, it would be utterly*
>   *scorned.*
>
> (Song of Songs 8:6-7)

We pray because God loves us and desires for us to be in communion with Him. Sharing our desires is a pathway to intimacy and connection.

We pray because it helps us see God's heart more clearly. It helps us to see that He is for us and that our pain is handled carefully and skillfully by His love. Though He does not always answer our prayers the way we would like for Him to, He always answers our deepest need.

> **We pray because it helps us see God's heart more clearly.**

What do *you* want Jesus to do for you? What are your needs or desires and your hopes?

Leaning into Hope

Jesus is the Only One who can truly satisfy our needs, desires, dreams, and hopes. The "why" of prayer is that it opens intimate communication between us and God.

We should find great encouragement from Jesus's question to these two blind men. He desires for us to share our hearts, admit our needs, and ask for help. He is eager to give us the help He knows is best.

God is not a heavenly slot machine—put the prayers in, pull the handle, and all your requests are granted. Jesus is more interested in the relationship than simply granting our requests.

God is not Santa Claus, a benevolent character who gives presents when we are good. He is more interested in the deeper needs beneath our surface needs, and He will always meet those because He is good. Not everyone receives physical healing, but all can receive inner healing.

God is not the Tooth Fairy, a gift giver only when we give something first. Instead, God is a loving Father who desires to give His children all they require. He could grant all our wishes, but sometimes His answer is "trust me," because He knows what is best for us and promises to fulfill the good plans He has for us. Knowing this helps us to see prayer as a relationship in which we're safe to communicate what we desire, trusting God will give us what we need.

What is your main goal in prayer? Why do you pray?

Do you believe God really wants to hear from you and that what you ask for matters to Him? Explain your response.

When have you prayed and God did not answer the way you wanted? How did that affect your feelings about God? Your prayer life?

How can you be more intentional in your prayer life?

Were you later able to see how God met a deeper need—perhaps one you were not even aware of at the time? And if so, how did that deepen your connection and intimacy with God?

A Practical Next Step

Some people use the acronym A.C.T.S. to remember an effective way to pray. Obviously, it is not the only one, but it is a great way to keep prayer in balance by focusing on relationship:

Adoration   Praise God for who He is and how great He is, including how much He loves you.

Confession   Admit the ways you have tried to live life your way, contrary to God's Word.

Thanksgiving   Thank God for all the blessings in your life.

Supplication   Ask God for the things you desire, including your deeper desires. Try it on for size for the next few days, shaping your prayers accordingly.

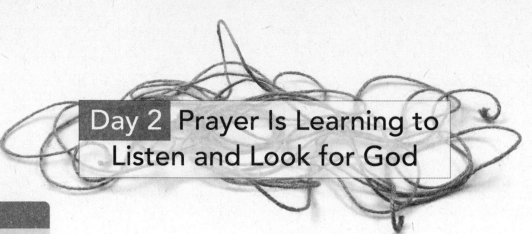

Day 2 Prayer Is Learning to Listen and Look for God

Big Idea

Prayer helps us hear and see God at work in our lives.

Jesus's Question:
"If I am telling the truth, why don't you believe me?"
(John 8:46)

The Question We Ask:
Why does it seem God isn't answering my prayer?

Leaning into the Question

Sincere prayer, in all its forms, springs from humility—the realization that we are not enough to fulfill our desires on our own and manage life's circumstances. In short, we are not in control. And when we are willing to humble ourselves and pray, trusting God, He proves Himself faithful in our lives to have the power not only to change our circumstances, but to change our hearts as well. Heart change is God's specialty, because God longs to be in loving relationship with us. There is beauty in admitting our inability to meet our own needs, our need for help, and our longing for love from our Creator.

In 1945, after World War II, L.S. "Sam" Shoen and his bride, Anna Mary Carty Shoen, recognized the need for do-it-yourself moving equipment that could be available for one-way journeys nationwide. They were disappointed to discover that such an opportunity was not available, so they chose to start a company themselves. And U-Haul was born.[1] Today this moving and storage company rents trucks, trailers, and other cargo vehicles to equip people across America to admit that they cannot handle all their junk without help.

When it comes to prayer, even when there is doubt, we have to admit to God and ourselves that we cannot handle the "junk" of life without His help. We must place our concerns, dreams, aspirations, and needs in the care of the most capable One—the one who cannot just move our junk, but move mountains if we ask Him to (Matthew 17:20-21). It is longing, looking, and seeking Jesus instead of looking to our own resources. Most of us are celebrated for self-sufficiency and autonomy, but in the case of faith, we are called to rely on God. Longing, looking, and seeking communicate not only humility but also a desire to trust God with our concerns.

I remember a day when I was desperately longing, looking, and seeking. I had never felt so panicked. I could feel my heartbeat as I made each phone call, frantically trying to locate my kids. I had dropped them off at the local outdoor mall for an hour to shop for Christmas gifts. They had exited the car with hopeful smiles, money in their pockets, and the elation fueled by the freedom and responsibility of shopping by themselves for the first time. Although our daughter was a teenager, our son was only ten, but both were certainly old enough for this shopping trip without incident, or so I thought.

I arrived at our designated meeting spot exactly one hour after I had dropped them off. Cars behind me honked; I was blocking their path, so I drove around a few times, checking my watch. *They are only six minutes late; maybe they are checking out and it's just taking longer,* I thought to myself. *They are only thirteen minutes late; maybe they stopped to get a frozen yogurt.* But my pretend scenarios got more and more pathetic and my "mom brain" got more and more frantic.

They did not have cell phones; in our house, one earns the right to have a cell phone when one gets a job at sixteen and can pay for it. It had sounded like a good decision when my husband and I had made it, but at that moment, when I could not find them, I questioned the wisdom of our policy.

I finally parked the car and briskly walked to our predetermined meeting place. After waiting a few minutes there, I could not stand it any longer and began walking through each store in the area, asking any salesperson I saw if he or she had seen my offspring. When I got to the end of the mall, I was desperate to find them. Every television episode I'd ever seen that had a storyline with missing children, both real and fictional, raced through my mind. I tried to shake off the thoughts that began to plague me—the things that could be happening, the horrors they might be facing.

I found a police officer and shared my plight. He was empathetic but also tried to calm me with platitudes. I didn't want platitudes; I wanted my kids. After almost two hours had passed, I drove home quickly to see if maybe they had gone home or left a message on our home phone. When I pulled into the driveway, my vehicle seemed to freeze in time. What if they weren't there? What would I do? My tears went from a sprinkle to a downpour and my cries echoed inside of my minivan. "Please, God. Please. Help me find them."

I finally found the strength to enter the house. It was empty. Emptier than it had ever felt to me before. I checked the kids' rooms and stayed long enough to smell the rooms, hoping for a scent of hope.

Then the phone rang. I could not get there fast enough. "Hello?"

"Mrs. Neese, this is Officer Charles from the Bakersfield Police Department; you and I spoke earlier at the mall. We have two kids here who say they belong to you and your husband."

My heart leaped in my chest. "May I speak to them?"

The tears returned, this time full of gratitude. I tried not to weep audibly as my daughter explained that she and her brother were invited to go to a movie with friends from church and that she had borrowed a classmate's cell phone to leave a message to let me know. Such a decision went against family rules, but right then all I wanted was to wrap my arms around those cuties. There would be plenty of time later to review family rules. I was overcome with gratitude to God and simply wanted to savor the moment of finding those I had been looking for and longing to embrace.

Mary Magdalene had spent her life longing, looking, and seeking. When examining her narrative in the Gospels, we find that Jesus cleansed her from seven demons who were plaguing her. Such a possession must have been arduous physically, spiritually, and emotionally. She must have been looking for some way out, some path to freedom (she may have even prayed). When Jesus came into her life, she found the One for whom she was longing, looking, and seeking. In turn, out of her gratitude for the cleansing, she was a devoted follower of Jesus, was His financial supporter, and was part of the travel entourage that sometimes accompanied Him.

> After this, Jesus traveled about from one town and village to another, proclaiming the good news of the kingdom of God. The Twelve were with him, ²and also some women who had been cured of evil spirits and diseases: Mary (called Magdalene) from whom seven demons had come out; ³Joanna the wife of Chuza, the manager of Herod's household; Susanna; and many others. These women were helping to support them out of their own means.
>
> (Luke 8:1-3)

On their journeys, Mary Magdalene must have seen Jesus heal the sick, raise the dead, feed the multitudes, and love others well. She has the distinct honor in history as being an eyewitness to both the crucifixion and burial of Jesus. Since He was the One who freed her from her possession, His death must have left her feeling depleted and devastated. All her dreams for the future must have been dashed on the rocks of Calvary.

But then Sunday came!

> ⁹When Jesus rose early on the first day of the week, he appeared first to Mary Magdalene, out of whom he had driven seven demons. ¹⁰She went and told those who had been with him and who were mourning and weeping. ¹¹When they heard that Jesus was alive and that she had seen him, they did not believe it.

[12]Afterward Jesus appeared in a different form to two of them while they were walking in the country. . . .

[20]Then the disciples went out and preached everywhere, and the Lord worked with them and confirmed his word by the signs that accompanied it.

(Mark 16:9-12, 20)

The women had just faced the worst day of their lives, watching Jesus crucified on Friday. It no doubt was a day filled with all sorts of emotions—fear, sadness, anger, disappointment, and frustration. But then they placed His body in the grave, a symbol of finality, and the guards placed a large stone in front of it.

No one knows why the women would try to care for a body that was clearly protected by a giant rock they could never move. Maybe they were looking for a glimpse of hope. Maybe they were looking for a glimmer of the purpose behind all the pain and loss they had endured. Going to the tomb to anoint the body made no earthly sense, but God is not limited to earthly confines.

We all have had seasons of uncertainty, days where we were unsure what to expect, but the women headed to the tomb on Easter morning were in for the most amazing and beautiful shock of their lives.

What we know is that when Mary Magdalene went to the grave that day, she was looking for Jesus. And she was the first person to lay eyes on Jesus after His resurrection! But she was so overwrought with grief and panic that she did not recognize Him. Mary was so overcome with emotion and despair that she didn't believe it when she saw the One for whom she was looking, Jesus.

Like Mary, often we do not have eyes to see God's answers to our prayers. Sometimes we perceive our prayers to be unanswered because the answer that comes does not look like what we think it should. For me, the answer to my prayer is often God's (perfect) timing, not my (impatient) timing, and so my prayer seems fruitless even when it is not. Can you relate? And let's just admit it: sometimes it seems unfair that while we're still waiting on God, others' prayers are answered—including the prayers of those who do not even know or believe in God.

As I am writing this, I am sitting in the same jeans I have worn for the last five days. On a weekend of four speaking engagements in Virginia, I left my home at 4 a.m. on the first day wearing a cute outfit (including crazy-cute yellow shoes and earrings) and carrying three packed bags. Somewhere between California and Virginia, my luggage was transported to and deposited in Las Vegas, but it never was forwarded on to the destination. I guess what happens in Vegas really *does* stay there!

In the one piece of luggage I had with me, I had workout clothes, some business cards, and a few books to sell.

> Sometimes we perceive our prayers to be unanswered because the answer that comes does not look like what we think it should.

I prayed that the Lord would answer my prayer and have the bags delivered to me. I spent much of the weekend on the phone with the airlines, borrowing things from my tour mates, filling out forms, and buying a few things at Target to get me through the weekend until my bags arrived.

I missed the opportunity to sell books to the folks in the audience during the weekend, but I will tell you how God answered my prayer: with community. The others on the tour and I grew closer through sharing; I felt so connected to them. I received empathy and extra prayers from the members of the audiences we served. I even got a few cute shirts that go with my sassy yellow shoes.

I, like Mary, thought the answer to my prayers would look a certain way. We both were mistaken. But we both were blessed with an answer that was more beautiful than we could have imagined.

If we are honest, often the things we long for and seek are about us—what we think we need and how we think the answers to those needs will look.

Mary's deepest desire was to see Jesus, but when He did not look like she thought He would, her heart was discouraged, clouding her ability to see Jesus clearly.

When was the last time you prayed to see God in your life?

When do you "see" God most clearly? How do you know it is Him?

When has God answered your prayers differently from how you hoped He would yet, in retrospect, you can see His hand in all of it?

Leaning into the Scripture

In John 8, we find more evidence that the Pharisees do not believe Jesus comes from God. Jesus's question and statement following his question highlight the importance of believing Him and trusting Him when it comes to every aspect of our relationship, especially prayer.

42Jesus said to them, "If God were your Father, you would love me, for I have come here from God. I have not come on my own; God sent me. 43Why is my language not clear to you? Because you are unable to hear what I say. 44You belong to your father, the devil, and you want to carry out your father's desires. He was a murderer from the beginning, not holding to the truth, for there is no truth in him. When he lies, he speaks his native language, for he is a liar and the father of lies. 45Yet because I tell the truth, you do not believe me! 46Can any of you prove me guilty of sin? **If I am telling the truth, why don't you believe me?** *47Whoever belongs to God hears what God says. The reason you do not hear is that you do not belong to God."*

(John 8:42-47, emphasis added)

In these verses, Jesus was articulating to the Pharisees His identity as God's Son. Those of us who call Him Lord can see what He is doing in this conversation with the religious leaders and be encouraged by his questions. We believe, and therefore we not only can see Him but also can hear Him (v. 47). Prayer increases our ability to hear God. As we get to know Jesus in prayer, we become more familiar with His voice and deepen our trust in Him. This intimacy enables us to "see" him more clearly in our lives as well.

How has prayer increased your ability to see and hear God?

Mary did not recognize Jesus when she saw Him. How do you recognize Jesus's activity in your life? How do you know it's Him?

The Pharisees heard Jesus's words but did not "hear" God. Jesus encourages us that because we believe, we can hear Him. When and how have you heard God? What does His voice "sound like" to you?

Leaning into Hope

With regard to prayer, I am encouraged that the more I seek Jesus's heart, way, will, and word—the more I seek *Him*—the more my prayers will begin to align with His desires for me and the more clearly I will both hear Him and see Him. The same is true for you. Prayer helps us to listen and look for God, and the beautiful result is that we hear and see Him at work in our lives more and more!

A Practical Next Step

Spend ten minutes today simply listening for God. It may be hard not to mentally make your grocery list or plan for dinner, but just sit in readiness to hear from God. When your mind wanders, simply return your focus to God by silently whispering "Jesus" or "Father." Set a timer and when it goes off, write down (or journal about) anything you heard.

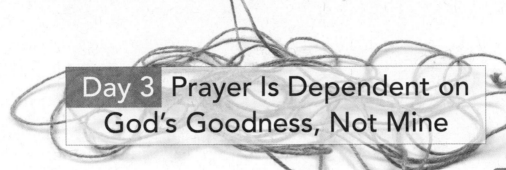

Day 3 Prayer Is Dependent on God's Goodness, Not Mine

Big Idea

God does not answer our prayers according to our behavior.

Jesus's Question:
Jesus answered, "Do you think that these Galileans were worse sinners than all the other Galileans because they suffered this way?"
(Luke 13:2)

The Question We Ask:
Does my righteousness (or lack thereof) affect whether or not God answers my prayers?

Leaning into the Question

Juliane Koepcke had no idea what the day after her high school graduation would look like. She and her mother boarded LANSA Flight 508 on Christmas Eve in 1971. The seventeen-year-old was traveling with her mother to spend Christmas with her father, a German zoologist from Peru. The flight was scheduled to be a little over an hour in duration but was caught in a massive thunderstorm. The motor was struck by a lightning bolt and the aircraft broke into numerous pieces. Juliane heard screams, realized she was free-falling from the sky strapped to her airplane seat, and then lost consciousness. She fell ten thousand feet into the Peruvian rain forest, and by the grace of God, only broke a collarbone, suffered a deep gash on her calf, received a cut above her eye, and endured a concussion.

She spent eleven days trying to find help. She discovered some expired passengers from the crash and survived off the sweets she found in their belongings.

During her search for rescue, she did hear rescue planes and helicopters, but through the thick rain forest canopy, they could not spot her.

On the ninth day of her journey, she came across three Peruvian forest workers who led her to a hospital. She soon discovered that she was the only survivor of the plane carrying ninety-two passengers.

Ninety-two other people were aboard that plane. No doubt some on the plane said (or screamed) prayers before plummeting to their deaths. But they did not live to see them answered.[2]

This tragic story raises some big questions: How? Why? What does that say about God? What does that say about us? What does that say about prayer? Perhaps it causes you to think of a

tragic situation that touched your own life and questions about why God didn't answer your own prayers or the prayers of others. Maybe you've wondered if your own behaviors, or those of others, were to blame, hindering your prayers.

Sometimes, the person who curses God lives a full, rich life and the preacher dies a young pauper. Haven't we all heard stories of missionaries killed by the very people they went to serve in Jesus's name? It is unfair in our eyes, but God has a higher perspective. These are bitter pills for us to swallow, and yet, we can trust that if God does not show favoritism in this way, His love really is unconditional.

Fortunately for us, the book of James gives us a little puzzle piece in the mystery of prayer:

> Make this your common practice: Confess your sins to each other and pray for each other so that you can live together whole and healed. The prayer of a person living right with God is something powerful to be reckoned with. Elijah, for instance, human just like us, prayed hard that it wouldn't rain, and it didn't—not a drop for three and a half years. Then he prayed that it would rain, and it did. The showers came and everything started growing again.
>
> (James 5:16-18 MSG)

According to these verses, our prayers should be practiced with a clear conscious so that our connection with God will be communal, restorative, healing, and powerful. Prayer is crazy powerful; however, prayer is powerful not because of our righteousness but because of the righteousness of God. We cannot cajole, manipulate, or strong-arm God with our good works.

In the Old Testament, the prophet Elijah had done the bidding of God for a long time. God did not repay his *behavior* with answered prayers, but God *did* answer his prayers. We're told Elijah was human—and therefore imperfect—just as we are. So, God did not answer Elijah's prayers because of his worthiness but because God values the cry of a fervent heart. I love the straightforward way one writer articulates it: "The power of prayer is proved from the history of Elijah. In prayer we must not look to the merit of man, but to the grace of God."[3]

Leaning into the Scripture

We see this theme of God's grace in Luke 13, where there is a discussion with Jesus about some Galileans and suffering. Although commentators are uncertain about the exact turn of events that precipitated these questions, one thing is clear: Jesus's questions cut right through the uncertainty to communicate a certain truth.

After Jesus was informed that some Galileans were killed when making sacrifices (v. 1), He responds with this question:

Jesus answered, "Do you think that these Galileans were worse sinners than all the other Galileans because they suffered this way?" (v. 2)

One commentator notes, "Jesus' point was not that the Galileans in question were innocent; His point was that they were simply not more guilty than the others. All were and are guilty."[4] The commentator goes on to say of verse 2 that many think "God should allow good things to happen to good people and bad things to bad people. [But] Jesus corrected this thinking."[5]

The good news in Jesus's question is that righteousness does not give us a "get whatever you want" card in prayer, but it does give us a sort of "get out of jail free card" when it comes to the forgiveness of God—*all because of the grace of Jesus.* No one deserves the grace Jesus bestows on those who accept Him, or the love for all those He has made. Yet God freely extends his love and grace.

I don't know about you, but in my flesh I tend not only to place people in the "good" or "bad" category but also to think God should allow good things to happen to those in the "good" category and not-so-good things to happen to the others—and to think that the prayers of the "good" carry more weight than those of the "bad." Jesus squashes this thinking with His question! Although the question does not directly address prayer, it does directly address the matter of our hearts.

- We all have compared ourselves to others.
- We all have missed the mark of righteousness.
- We all have prayed, using our good deeds as prayer leverage to try and talk God into believing we deserve whatever we are asking for.
- We all have gone our own way.
- We all, on some level, have been prodigals—even if we did not have to eat pig slop to recognize it.
- We all have fallen short of the glory of God (Romans 3:23).
- We all are guilty of messing up, choosing to go our own way, and putting ourselves first.

The reality of our hearts leads us to God's grace and the hope we have in Jesus! And this brings us back to the common question of whether righteousness (or the lack thereof) affects God's answer to our prayers.

Many religions are based on the formula of "do good and get good stuff." If you complete a task list of good deeds, somehow you will win the favor of a deity. As believers in Jesus, it is easy to fall into the trap of thinking that we can manipulate the goodness and power of God by doing good works. It's the mindset that if we behave well, good things will happen to us and our prayers will be answered.

Jesus's question in Luke 13 clearly states that Jesus is not interested in human formulas for getting what we want—in being religious for the benefits. He knows that all fall short of the standards of a holy God. He also knows that prayer is

not contingent on anything other than the goodness of God. Although the prayer offered up by the righteousness "avails much" (James 5:16 NKJV), God cannot be manipulated by our acts of goodness.

> **What have you done in the past to try to win favor with God or others? How did that work for you?**

> **What do your prayers reveal about how you believe prayer "works"? Is it difficult for you to accept that God's answers to your prayers are not determined by your behavior? Why or why not?**

We can find hope in the fact that God knows we are guilty of disobedience yet still hears our prayers because of His great love and unlimited grace.

Leaning into Hope

We can find hope in the fact that God knows we are guilty of disobedience yet still hears our prayers because of His great love and unlimited grace. This is why He sent His Son, Jesus, to die for our sins. Regardless of our behavior, God hears our prayers! And God responds to our prayers according to *His* goodness and righteousness. If this is hard to swallow, just consider these men from scripture:

- The apostle Paul, who penned much of the New Testament, was once a ruthless crusader who was determined to thwart the spread of the gospel and even oversaw the killing of early Christians (Acts 22:4).
- King David has been called a man after God's own heart, but he, among other things, was guilty of murder (2 Samuel 11:17; 12:9), telling lies (2 Samuel 11:7-8, 12-13), coveting a neighbor's wife (2 Samuel 11:3), committing adultery (2 Samuel 11:4), and stealing the wife of another (2 Samuel 12:9). If there was a sin punch card, he would have earned a free yogurt or two.
- Jonah, famous for being a prophet who was swallowed by a whale, showed blatant disregard for God's commands to go to Nineveh and preach to the people there (Jonah 1:1-3).

These men—all used by God in mighty ways to tell the story of redemption, grace, and mercy—were all imperfect. Yet their imperfection did not disqualify them from being loved, heard, and used by God.

We, too, can be billboards for God's story of redemption, grace, and mercy. He can use even our imperfections to draw both us and others closer to Him. And when we recall and realize just how much He has saved us from, our prayer lives are bolstered!

Here's the bottom line: God does not answer our prayers according to our behavior. (Can I get a hallelujah?) While an admirable trait, our righteousness brings no guarantee that God will answer our prayers. The truth is "all have sinned and fall short of the glory of God" (Romans 3:23) and all righteousness is imparted to us by God through Christ. So, although "the prayer of a righteous person is powerful and effective" (James 5:16), our lack of righteousness does not disqualify us from the favor of God. *Thanks be to God!*

When you don't see God answering your prayers, what is your response?

___ I build a case in my mind as to why He should answer them.

___ I list in my mind the things I have done for Him to "build my case."

___ I think that having an honest conversation with God about my religiosity will change things for me.

___ Other:

What roles do humility and confession play in your prayer life?

What did you glean about prayer from today's lesson?

A Practical Next Step

Prayerfully consider if any "formulas"—whether intentional or unintentional, known or unknown—have been influencing your prayer life. Consider if you have ever operated by this kind of mentality:

"If I _____, then God will _____."

Ask God to shine light on any false beliefs you have had about prayer. How is God inviting you to embrace His grace more fully as you pray and live?

Day 4 Prayer Reveals the Desires of My Heart

Big Idea

Prayer helps us understand and desire God's way.

Jesus's Question:
[53]*"Do you think I cannot call on my Father, and he will at once put at my disposal more than twelve legions of angels?* [54]*But how then would the Scriptures be fulfilled that say it must happen in this way?"*
(Matthew 26:53-54)

The Question We Ask:
Is prayer about more than getting what I want?

Leaning into the Question

I love to drive. Seriously. If my old knees did not make me stop every few hours to bend and stretch, and gas/food/bathrooms were not a necessity, I would drive cross-country without stopping. Give me some iced tea, a few million sunflower seeds, a great soundtrack or book in the speakers, and I am one happy clam.

Except when there are semi-trucks around. No offense to the hard-working truckers who transport goods across the country every day and night, but they kind of stress me out. Their rigs are much bigger than my car and have up to thirty-four tires that can cause road hazards.

I have noticed in my travels, however, that some of the vehicular behemoths have eye-catching designs—spikes on the wheels and other designs, especially plastic arrows on the wheels. I have often wondered about these arrows. Do they have a purpose?

These brightly colored bits of plastic on wheel lugs actually serve a purpose: they are loose wheel-nut indicators. They communicate to the driver when the wheel's lug nuts are coming loose. Lug nuts are important safeguards; they help fasten a tire to the vehicle's axle. With much mileage, age, and use, they become looser, less secure, and increasingly dangerous. Wheels with the arrow design allow the driver to identify quickly when they are no longer secure.

I wish my mouth had a similar feature when I come home after a weekend of speaking and my house looks like my family had a garage sale while I was gone.

How do you recognize when your emotional and/or spiritual lug nuts have loosened?

When I get too big for my britches, rely too heavily on my own power, or think I deserve God to answer my prayers, there are no arrows to point out my issues. But in those seasons, I do more

bargaining and less trusting in prayer. I tend to focus more on my challenges and my plans than on Christ and His purposes.

When we are in the right frame of heart and mind, we do not pray to get our way, we pray to better understand God's way.

There is an often-quoted verse about our heart's desires: "Take delight in the Lord, and he will give you the desires of your heart" (Psalm 37:4). Oftentimes, I find myself celebrating and counting on the second part of that verse without focusing on the first and more important part.

I want the desires of my heart. A bigger bank account, more time with my family, a maid, more vacations, the ability to eat whatever I want without consequences, a book on *The New York Times* Best Seller list, perfect health, and confidence in a bathing suit. Those things will probably never happen, but that does not stop me from desiring them. But looking at the preceding verses helps my perspective.

> *Do not fret because of those who are evil*
> *or be envious of those who do wrong;*
> *for like the grass they will soon wither,*
> *like green plants they will soon die away.*
>
> *Trust in the Lord and do good;*
> *dwell in the land and enjoy safe pasture.*
> *Take delight in the Lord,*
> *and he will give you the desires of your heart.*
>
> (Psalm 37:1-4)

There is much to unpack here. In my journal, I decided to write these verses and "translate" them into Amberly-ese (my language):

- "Do not fret because of those who are evil." — Trust God to be just.
- "[do not] be envious of those who do wrong." — Do not look at the path of others but do right.
- "Trust in the Lord." — Know God and put all your faith in Him.
- ". . . and do good." — Make the right decisions by keeping your eyes on Him.
- "Enjoy safe pasture." — Rest in the protection of God, the Good Shepherd.
- "Take delight in the Lord." — Find joy, purpose, and meaning in Him, not in material things.
- ". . . and he will give you the desires of your heart." — When you are focused on God, He will exchange and improve your list of wants.

My translation is far inferior to the original text, but sometimes such an exercise helps me grasp the concepts more readily. In short,

- the more I know God, the more I love Him;
- the more I love Him, the more I trust Him;
- the more I trust Him, the more I understand that His plans are better than mine; and
- the more I understand that, the more the desires of my heart echo the desires of His heart for me.

Prayer reveals the desires of our hearts and aligns our desires with God's.

This is what prayer does for us—it reveals the desires of our hearts and aligns our desires with God's. Just like friends who spend a lot of time together often start dressing more alike and using similar expressions, when we spend more time with God and listen to what He says, it transforms us and aligns our hearts more with His.

Leaning into the Scripture

Jesus serves as the perfect example of Psalm 37, especially when His time on earth is dwindling down. There are plenty of people doing evil all around Him, many of whom want Him dead. Jesus keeps His eyes on His Father, and by praying honestly in the garden of Gethsemane (Matthew 26:36-46), He is able to know and affirm and eventually yield to what His Father wanted—to reconcile humanity to Himself through Jesus.

When His friend Judas betrays Him (talk about doing evil!), Jesus points to the plan of God instead of saving His own neck (Matthew 26:42). And when another of Jesus's friends tries to fight back in the garden when the soldiers come to arrest Him, Jesus reminds him of the plan:

> [53]*"Do you think I cannot call on my Father, and he will at once put at my disposal more than twelve legions of angels? [54]But how then would the Scriptures be fulfilled that say it must happen in this way?"*
>
> (Matthew 26:53-54)

As a reminder, those in attendance would have been familiar with the stories of God providing for His people (Exodus 16) and fighting for His people (Exodus 14). Jesus reminds us in this passage that God is able not only to fight our battles but also to provide for the desires of our hearts.

But when Jesus asked, *"Do you think I cannot call on my Father, and he will at once put at my disposal more than twelve legions of angels?"* I think it goes deeper than just asking if they think God can, but instead, when things get hairy, *will He?* Does He hear the prayers of His Son? The prayers of His people?

But these questions actually reveal much, not only about God's capability of protecting us but also about Jesus's desire to do the will of God. His ultimate desire (even though it meant arrest, beating, crucifixion, sweating blood, denial by some of His followers, and death) was to fulfill the Scriptures and reconcile the world to God through His sacrifice. Jesus's heart was to submit to the plans of God and set an example for us to do likewise.

Leaning into Hope

God wants what's best for us, and although He can accomplish what is best without us, He wants us to know him, trust Him, join Him in His work, and enjoy a loving relationship with Him. This happens as we let go of our own agendas in prayer and come to understand and desire God's way—which is always for our good and the good of the world. As a result, we come to look more and more like Jesus.

So, how can we let go of our own agendas like Jesus did? How do we begin to understand and desire God's way and trust it is for our good?

- First, we seek His face and get to know Him more intimately (Jeremiah 29:13).
- We study God's word for teaching, correction, and instruction (2 Timothy 3:16).
- We seek to know His will through wisdom and understanding (Colossians 1:9).
- We pray that we may hear from Him more clearly and trust Him more fully (Jeremiah 33:3).
- And then, just as Jesus set His agenda aside for the plans of His Father, we choose to do so more regularly (Psalm 119:30).

How do you look more like Jesus today than you did five to ten years ago? How do you hope to look more like Jesus five to ten years from now?

Name three "desires of your heart."

1.

2.

3.

Think of what the "desires of your heart" might have looked like when you were five. Or fifteen. Or twenty-five. How have those desires changed? What brought about the change?

What do you sense the desires of God's heart are for you?

A Practical Next Step

Read all of Psalm 37. How do the promises found in this psalm shape how you feel about prayer—about being still before God and waiting on Him (v. 7)? Which of the promises are you most excited about? Why?

Now, meditate on verse 4: "Take delight in the Lord, and he will give you the desires of your heart." Talk with God about this verse and how it connects with your experience of God in this season. Are you delighting in God? Why or why not? What are the desires of your heart, and what does God have to say to you about them?

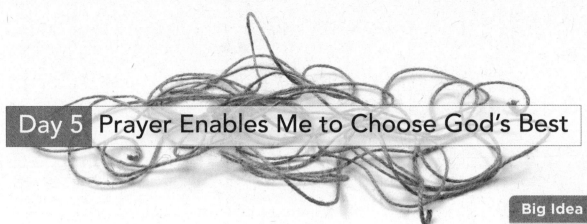

Day 5 Prayer Enables Me to Choose God's Best

Jesus's Question:
"Did not the Messiah have to suffer these things and then enter his glory?"
(Luke 24:26)

The Question We Ask:
Am I willing to lay down my agenda for God's?

Leaning into the Question

I could not take my eyes off her boots. I was at Sky Harbor Airport, about to board a plane. I was positioned at a standing lunch counter; seating is so limited that there are only a few tables with chairs; the rest are counters designed for standing patrons to eat at like a human trough.

An impeccably dressed woman was seated by herself, and although she was certainly beautiful, it was her cowboy boots that were really spectacular. I could *not* keep from saying something to her.

As I threw away my lunch remnants, I passed by her table and softly said, "I love your boots."

"*Excuse me?*" she responded with a voice anything but soft.

"Ummm . . . your boots," I responded sheepishly. "I think they are amazing."

"Oh, my *boots*," she laughed. "I am so sorry I was rude. Will you forgive me?"

She asked me to sit down. After exchanging pleasantries, she explained why she had been so defensive about my compliment. She had breast cancer that led to a double mastectomy. She had survived the cancer, but it had left her feeling disfigured.

After years of feeling a bit "deformed" (her words, not mine), her friends finally talked her into getting reconstructive surgery. Her body may have looked more complete, but the procedure left her feeling hyper-sensitive.

So, when a stranger in an airport made a comment about her *boots*, she misheard the compliment and thought I was judging her "top shelf" (which has a slang term that sounds a lot like "boots").

We laughed about it, and then the subject changed to what we do for a living. We discovered that we are both Christian authors (she actually wrote a book I read to my kids at least once a

week for two years). I was thankful that I had arrived at the airport early and had time to converse with this kindred spirit.

Her last question to me, after we exchanged contact information, was to find out if I had any dreams I had not had the guts to explore.

"I would love to try comedy someday," I responded. "But I am too chicken."

Two weeks later, I received a call I will never forget. It was from a very famous and successful comedian. She explained that a good friend of hers (my new boots friend) had passed my contact information along and encouraged her to connect with me. She explained that she had about thirty minutes until she needed to leave her hotel room for a comedy show and that I could ask her anything about getting into comedy.

I cried—though I tried to hide my excitement, listen to her feedback, and pick her brain to the best of my ability. I am thankful to say that this comedian is a personal friend today. Our conversation was absolutely the genesis of my finding the guts to explore comedy more fully. Although it was over twenty years ago, it still makes me mist up when I think that it all started with cowboy boots and a funeral.

Oh wait, I forgot to tell you. I was in that airport on that day because I had officiated the funeral of a family member earlier that day. The conversation with a stranger that led to a relationship with my new comedian friend would not have been possible without the loss of someone I loved.

The same is true with Jesus. In order for our relationship with God to be born, Jesus had to die. For us to have real life, Jesus had to suffer a real death. For us to have unrestricted access to talk with God in prayer, Jesus's body had to be restricted to a cross with nails. What lengths God was willing to go to to ensure we could have a relationship with Him! Only in God's economy does loss equal gain, but aren't we thankful it does?

Although we addressed the Lord's Prayer (Matthew 6:9-13) in an earlier lesson (Week 1, Day 1, we would be remiss not to revisit it this week as we focus on prayer. One of the most difficult aspects of the Lord's Prayer is forgiveness, and forgiveness involves loss.

For true forgiveness to happen, our agendas, our bitterness, our will, our pride, our need to be right, and our selfishness need to "die" so that forgiveness can "live." Fortunately for us, Jesus set many beautiful examples of self-sacrifice, chief of all his death on the cross.

Leaning into the Scripture

After his death and resurrection, Jesus appeared to two of His followers; they had not seen the risen Christ yet and were confused and sad that He was not to be found in the tomb. Jesus addressed their sadness and reminded them of the greater plan. His question to them wrote them a reality check: "Did not the Messiah have to suffer these things and then enter his glory?" (Luke 24:26).

Jesus was reminding these two men of God's plan for redeeming His children. Jesus came to earth to suffer so that imperfect humans could be reconciled to a perfect God. He came to bridge the gap between a God who can answer prayer and a people who need Him.

Jesus's work on the cross grants us hope, forgiveness, grace, and so much more, but it required His sacrifice and suffering. It required Jesus to lay down all other agendas so that the agenda of God could be fully realized. When we pray, we need to be willing to do the same thing—lay down our agendas for the agendas of God.

When I first started dating in my teens, I was always amazed at the gentlemen who would ask, "What would *you* like to do?"

When I grew in my prayer life, I grew to understand that prayer certainly invites us to say to the Lord, "What would *you* like to do in me? What would *you* like to do in this situation? This is the goal of all prayer, sacrificing our agenda for God's.

> When we pray, we need to be willing to lay down our agendas for the agendas of God.

Read the story of the two followers encountering Jesus on the road to Emmaus (Luke 24:13-27). How do you think their own agendas might have prevented them from recognizing not only Jesus but also God's plan of redemption? In what ways can you relate to these two followers?

Why is it so difficult for us to sacrifice our agenda for God's agenda? What is something you are struggling to surrender to God in prayer now? What are your concerns or fears related to this person or situation? Share your heart honestly with God in the space below:

Leaning into Hope

Is sacrificing our agenda hard? Yes! But as we have seen in Jesus's own example, suffering is often part of the faith equation when we pray. So, how do we do it? We ask Jesus to help us. We share vulnerably with God, being real and raw about our concerns and fear and hesitations, knowing that He understands our humanity and will be patient and gentle with us. He will send the Comforter, the Advocate, the Holy Spirit to help us in our weakness as we pray, interceding for us with "groanings too deep for words" (Romans 8:26 NASB).

When we find ourselves wanting what we want in prayer, we can remind ourselves that prayer is not just asking God for things; it is bringing our concerns

and desires to the God who loves us with abandon and laying them at His feet, surrendering our agenda so that we may receive His. And the beautiful thing is that when we drop our agendas at the feet of God, our hands and arms are open to receive the good plans He has for us! When we acquiesce our agenda for God's agenda in prayer, He works powerfully in our lives, doing "immeasurably more than all we can ask or imagine" (Ephesians 3:20). He gives us abundant life. He gives us meaningful purpose. And best of all, He gives us Himself—with all the fullness of life and power that comes from His love, a love that is longer, wider, higher, and deeper than we can possibly fathom (Ephesians 3:18).

After a week of looking at prayer, how would you explain prayer to someone unfamiliar with it?

Why do you think so many of us struggle to drop our agendas at the feet of Jesus?

What does it mean to you to have access to a relationship with God through prayer?

A Practical Next Step

Take ten minutes and write down all the prayer requests that come to mind. What might it look like for you to lay down your agenda as you lift up these concerns so that you can make room for God's agenda and power in answering these requests? Rather than bombarding God with specific requests, spend time in silence as you lift up each need, asking the Holy Spirit to direct your prayers. How are you guided to pray more generally, rather than specifically? How does this challenge you?

Here's a prayer schedule that a friend and I created almost thirty years ago, and I have used it ever since to organize my prayers. Perhaps having a prayer schedule that helps to organize your prayers can enable you to pray with fewer words and more openness to how the Spirit might lead you to pray for each group/individual.

As you conclude praying for each one, leave your prayers at the feet of Jesus, acquiescing to His agenda and trusting in His power.

Monday	**M**issionaries, Church Leaders, Political Leaders
Tuesday	Those **T**roubled in Spirit
Wednesday	Those who Are **W**eak in Health
Thursday	**T**hankfulness
Friday	**F**riends and family
Saturday	**S**alvation
Sunday	**S**elf

Week 3 Wrap-up

I love giving gifts, not just because it sounds altruistic but because I really love it. The actual purchase of the gift is fun, but my favorite component of gift-giving is the mystery. I look at it like a crime to be solved. I gather evidence, conduct an informal survey of what the person already has, keep a notebook (all year long), listen for clues, and then do a significant deep dive for bargains (this investigator is on a budget).

I came from a family where one's Christmas list served as a shortcut; each person made a list of all he or she wanted and those buying gifts could use that to satisfy the list and the recipient.

My husband came from a family where a list was made by each person, but often, because his mom was so good at surprises, she would avoid the list so that a surprise could occur. This was fun for her, but it became a source of contention for my husband. When we got married, he admitted to consciously avoiding putting some stuff on his list so that his chance of receiving it increased.

I am sorry—*what?* That doesn't compute with my gift-giving bent.

One of the first gifts I ever bought him was a 6 CD changer for his car. Yes, kids, a CD changer. Now, CD players are relics, but at the time, a player that held numerous discs was both cutting-edge and a little pricey. But I scraped together as many shekels as possible and purchased the player. And then I had to wait for Christmas morning. When he opened the box, he was speechless. After much cajoling, he finally admitted that, initially, he was silent because he knew how much I had spent, but mostly he was pleasantly surprised because the gift was something he never dreamed would be under the tree.

Of course, due to a limited budget and time, I cannot always give every person in my life their "6 CD changer" gift, but I sure love trying.

Sometimes, we ask for things that would not be best for us. I know I have. Makeup at eight. A car at twelve. The captain of the football team at fourteen. And fifteen. And sixteen. Sometimes, we are like a child who lives on the fourth floor of a small New York apartment building who asks for a pony, but does not understand the ramifications of our wish being satisfied.

The same can be true of our prayers to God. God is sovereign and knows what's best. We are finite and do not. God is the perfect gift giver (James 1:17), because God loves us and wants what's best for us—most of all an intimate relationship with Him. As we've seen this week, prayer is about asking and trusting, petitioning and practicing patience. And perhaps most of all, leaning into the gifts of love and grace God has for us in the present moment.

When it comes to prayer, the important thing is to connect with God and share our hearts with vulnerability and authenticity.

> **When it comes to prayer, the important thing is to connect with God and share our hearts with vulnerability and authenticity.**

Of the questions we've explored, which one resonates most, and why?

What questions do you still have about prayer?

Read the week's memory verse, 1 John 5:14, slowly several times. Is there a word or phrase that catches your attention or touches your heart? What does God have to say to you about the word or phrase in light of your current life experience? How is God inviting you to respond?

How Can I Grow in My Faith?

Memory Verse:

1 John 5:14 NIV

Confidence:

This is the _____ we have in _____ God…

Caveat:

…according to _____ _____

Covenant:

…he _____ us.

Permission Slip:

This week, we took a long look at prayer—entrusting God with the desires of our hearts. Because God loves us and wants what's best for us—most of all, an intimate relationship with Him. Prayer is about asking and trusting, petitioning and practicing patience, and leaning into the gifts of love and grace God has for us right now. It is being in relationship with the God who loves us and coming to know God's heart more clearly and fully.

You have permission to _____.

"Call to me and I will answer you and tell you
great and unsearchable things you do not know."
(Jeremiah 33:3 NIV)

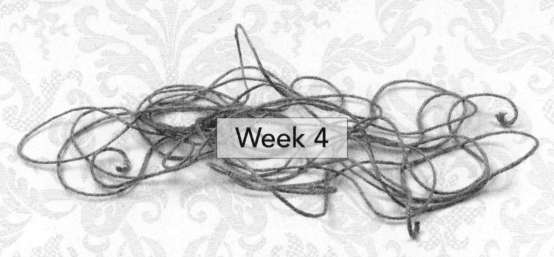

Week 4

What Must I Do to Be Healed?

Praise the Lord, my soul,
and forget not all his benefits—
who forgives all your sins
and heals all your diseases,
who redeems your life from the pit
and crowns you with love and compassion.

(Psalm 103:2-4)

I went almost nineteen years without breaking a bone.

In my sophomore year of college, I signed up for intramural football, a coed competition with students from my university. Although I am a huge football fan, I had not played except at the local schoolyard when I was in elementary school. But I had played soccer for many years and had developed a very strong kicking foot. So, when I signed up for the intramural team, I told the coach I wanted to be the kicker.

Not everyone on the team was excited to have a girl as the kicker; there were some men who could not believe a female was up for such a task. But once I showed them my abilities as a kicker—and my lack as a runner—I was given the position.

One of the guys on the team thought it best to use his foot as a football tee. Having played soccer, I had never used a tee before, so I objected. But he insisted, and I finally caved.

By the grace of God, when I kicked the ball, it flew deep into the territory of our opponent. But most of the momentum transpired between my foot and the foot of the "human tee." As a result, my strong kick broke my big toe and the two toes beside it, along with his pinky toe and the two toes beside it!

I had never experienced such pain before. With every step (or even thought of a step), pain shot through my foot to my leg and straight to my soul. WOW. I never thought I would heal. Weeks later, I still walked like Yoda and cringed that this had happened because I did not listen to my own objections. Healing seemed to take forever, although it was only six weeks, but my football days were over forever.

Healing comes in all shapes and sizes—whether it is physical, mental, emotional, or spiritual. Healing might look like a mended bone or a cured ailment, or it might look like a reconciled relationship, mental relief, or restored emotional strength. If you are not currently challenged with a wound of some kind, you will be. That's part of being human. But there is hope—as we will see this week in our exploration of healing from a biblical perspective through the lens of questions Jesus asked.

If you have been waiting for healing for a while, take heart! You are not alone. There are many examples in the scriptures of people who were waiting on healing, but one of my favorites is Sarah, the wife of Abraham. Sarah was barren in a time when a woman's value was squarely tied to her ability to conceive. So we might say that the healing she desired was not only physical but also emotional, mental, and even spiritual.

After God promised Abraham that he and Sarah would have a child, Sarah waited eleven years and then grew impatient; God wasn't healing on her time line. So, she decided to take matters into her own hands, giving her servant to Abraham to conceive and bear a child. This plan had major ramifications, including the heartbreaking reality that Sarah still did not have a child of her own. Despite her lack of trust in God, God allowed Sarah and Abraham to have a child twenty-four years after He had promised these two AARPers that they would be parents. Sarah saw firsthand how God can heal and restore us in every way we need.

We're often like Sarah, losing sight of God's promises and trying to fix things ourselves. But only God can bring the healing we need. God is the author of all healing, though sometimes that healing may not look like what we envision. While God does not promise physical healing in every instance, God always works to bring healing and wholeness within us, conforming us to the image of Jesus.

If you need healing, or know someone who does, this week will shine light on God's healing power and loving desire to restore your soul in Jesus.

Day 1 The Path to Healing Requires Humility

Big Idea

Healing is not dependent on our goodness or behavior.

Jesus's Question:
Jesus straightened up and asked her,
"Woman, where are they? Has no one condemned you?"
(John 8:10)

The Question We Ask:
Am I worthy of healing?

Leaning into the Question

Following the outbreak of the COVID-19 pandemic, those in ministry positions had to do some fancy footwork to pivot and continue ministry during periods of mandated or encouraged isolation. While some churches continued to have in-person services, many closed or transitioned to an online platform to preach the gospel and encourage listeners.

During an online sermon, a member of the British clergy, Vicar Stephen Beach of St Budeaux Parish Church, got more than he had anticipated. While he was delivering a message, he leaned too close to a candle on a cross. While he was articulating the heart of the message, the flame jumped from the candle to his sweater. He had asked his congregation to reflect on the message of waiting. During the final part of the sermon he delivered that week, he was encouraging his congregation members to wait on the Lord.

The man of God encouraged those watching, "It's a great thing to pause in the presence of God and to ask the question: Lord God, what are you saying to us?" He continued, "And then, of course, to wait for an answer. I've just been pausing between these . . ." he said before recognizing that his left shoulder was too close to the flame. Then he exclaimed, "Oh dear, I just caught on fire." He began to attempt to put out the flame. "Oh my word."[1]

The incident went viral on social media, and the vicar could not have predicted how the episode could have boosted awareness about the church. But he was most surprised by the response from his grandkids: "My family love it, and the youngest grandchildren want to know when Granddad is going to set himself on fire again."[2]

There are people in this world who believe that if one does the will of God, there will be no obstacles, no problems. That is simply not true. This vicar was encouraging his congregation to wait patiently on the Lord. He was doing good in the name of Jesus, and yet it did not disqualify him from a mishap—or having to purchase a new sweater. His little mistake made a big impact as the video of his fire—and his embarrassment—spread like wildfire (pun intended).

No doubt the vicar learned something about humility that day! However, a ruined sweater is a far different thing than a more serious hardship such as abuse, violence, disease, or loss. Every single day, in every country, on every continent, people die in car accidents, succumb to cancer, suffer from depression, endure abuse, lose a child, and are victims of violent crime. And those of us who love and serve God are not exempt from any form of suffering.

Though tithing, going to church, attending Bible study, and teaching Sunday school are all good things, they do not guarantee us a pass from illness, discomfort, or challenge. We live in a broken world where sin and sickness are realities for all. Yet many of us still struggle to understand why God would allow such bad things to happen, especially to those who are trying to serve Him well. It's an age-old question, one I've grappled with myself. How about you?

I'm not going to attempt to plumb the depths of that question today, though I encourage you to talk vulnerably with God about it. He understands our humanity and welcomes our grappling. What I want to explore today is this good news: Just as being in Christ does not shield us from hardship, so being sinful does not disqualify us from the healing touch of Jesus. In other words, our healing is not dependent on our behavior. Jesus desires for all to experience healing and wholeness in Him.

Though it is not one of the healing miracles, the story of the woman accused of adultery shows us that regardless of our past or present circumstances, all of us are eligible for Jesus's forgiveness—and Jesus's forgiveness opens us to His healing power in our lives.

Leaning into the Scripture

In John 8, we meet this woman accused of adultery and dragged to Jesus by the religious leaders, who wanted to trap Jesus using her indiscretion as the bait.

> [2]At dawn he appeared again in the temple courts, where all the people gathered around him, and he sat down to teach them. [3]The teachers of the law and the Pharisees brought in a woman caught in adultery. They made her stand before the group [4]and said to Jesus, "Teacher, this woman was caught in the act of adultery. [5]In the Law Moses commanded us to stone such women. Now what do you say?" [6]They were using this question as a trap, in order to have a basis for accusing him.

But Jesus bent down and started to write on the ground with his finger. [7]When they kept on questioning him, he straightened up and said to them, "Let any one of you who is without sin be the first to throw a stone at her." [8]Again he stooped down and wrote on the ground.

[9]At this, those who heard began to go away one at a time, the older ones first, until only Jesus was left, with the woman still standing there. [10]Jesus straightened up and asked her, "Woman, where are they? Has no one condemned you?"

[11]"No one, sir," she said.

"Then neither do I condemn you," Jesus declared. "Go now and leave your life of sin."

(John 8:2-11)

This story always stirs up mixed emotions for me because I can relate to all the characters.

I can relate to the woman caught in adultery. I certainly have made my fair share of poor choices and have felt shame and judgment for them. Although my sins might look different from hers, I can relate to feeling vulnerable and ashamed. She was dragged through the streets by religious leaders with her sinful choice being put on display for all to see.

I also can relate to the religious leaders. The Pharisees who pompously paraded this woman through the streets had judgment in their hearts and an agenda on their schedule—to trap Jesus. If He let the woman go, he would be ignoring the law of Moses, which required stoning for the sin of adultery. But if He condemned her, He would be violating Roman law, which stipulated that someone could be sentenced to death only by a judge. Jesus did not have the authority to sentence her to death. So the Pharisees were using the woman as a pawn in their strategic game of religiosity, hoping Jesus would join them in their judgment of the woman.

I have judged others before. It is usually when I am not spending enough time in God's Word, remembering who He is and who am I as His beloved. It is hard to act like anything other than a princess—a daughter of the King—when I am spending enough time with the King of kings. However, when I am feeling disconnected from the Truth, I often resort to puffing myself up by comparing myself with others or belittling others with judgment, even if only in my heart. Though I have never dragged anyone through any actual streets of judgment, I certainly have done so in my heart by gossiping.

I also can relate to Jesus in this story. When the power of His Holy Spirit is at work in me, I can show glimpses of the heart of Christ in my actions. I have extended undeserved favor to another. I have responded

in love when others have shown disdain. I have chosen the high road. It does not always happen, but it has occurred.

When I researched what commentators have to say about this story in preparation for writing my devotional book *The Friendship Initiative: 31 Days of Loving and Connecting Like Jesus*, I was frustrated by so many different thoughts regarding what Jesus might have written in the sand, because I'd love to know exactly what He wrote. But as I reread and visualized the scene in my mind, I realized that Jesus took a posture of humility not once but twice in this chapter (in verses 2 and 6)—He sat down to teach, and He bent down to write in the sand.

Instead of being concerned about *what* He wrote, I came to recognize the likelihood of why He bent down. Perhaps in humility, Jesus wanted to get on the level of those He was teaching to show value to each one, including the woman caught in adultery. Despite her impropriety, He desired spiritual healing for her and wanted to point her to grace.

After Jesus asked those without sin to cast the first stone, the onlookers began to walk away one by one. I can relate to them too. My own sinfulness reminds me that I have no right to judge others. I can only imagine the woman's relief when the stones began to fall. Obsessed with maintaining a facade of superiority and status, the religious leaders and onlookers dropped their pride and stones at the same time and walked away.

Jesus had every right to condemn her, but instead he reached out in kindness and asked, *"Woman, where are they? Has no one condemned you?"* (John 8:10).

This woman, by the letter of the Law, could have died on that day, but instead, Jesus saved her life. Jesus chose grace. He chose humility. He chose to offer healing for her soul.

Maybe that is why she addressed him as "Lord" after he spoke to her. Although we do not know the rest of her story, here we see her go from public humiliation to personal humility as she reverenced Jesus in this simple way. Perhaps in this moment she grasped the gravity of what had occurred. Although Jesus did not visibly heal her, he attended to her deepest needs by offering her forgiveness. And accepting the forgives of Jesus is the greatest healing of all!

With His forgiveness, Jesus encouraged the woman to go and be something better. In fact, His forgiveness and grace may have led to her spiritual healing and a change in her behavior. We don't know what happened after Jesus forgave her, but no doubt the love of Jesus impacted her greatly.

Jesus desires for *all* to experience healing and wholeness in Him. Aren't we thankful that healing, in its various forms, is available to us regardless of our background, behaviors, or battles? Just as right behavior does not exclude us from suffering, so our bad behavior does not exclude us from healing. It bears repeating: *healing is not dependent on our behavior.*

> Jesus desires for *all* to experience healing and wholeness in Him.

In light of the way Jesus treated the adulterous woman, how are you being invited to view your own struggles?

What can we learn from Jesus's example in this story about how to respond to someone who has fallen?

Do you have a friend who needs to hear that their healing is not dependent on their goodness? How might you encourage them?

Leaning into Hope

We are loved by God not for what we do, but because we are His. We are forgiven by God through the sacrifice of His Son, and "by his wounds we are healed" (Isaiah 53:5). Even so, we are called to a life of holiness—to "go and sin no more." Though you and I do not hear the verbiage "go and sin no more" in our conversations today, we can receive these words of Jesus as loving guidance for our own lives. Jesus calls us to holiness but loves us even when we fall far from that mark.

Knowing that our good behavior is not a requirement for forgiveness but a response to it, we can seek to live a life of freedom, health, and holiness in Christ—as well as come alongside others and encourage them to do the same. Though we live in a broken world where illness, ailments, disorders, and challenges occur, we can take heart that Jesus is with us and can use our suffering—and even our sins—to draw us to Him and redirect us, leading us on a path to healing and wholeness.

Have you ever heard Jesus's words "Go and sin no more" used in a hurtful way? If so, explain briefly.

Who in your life needs to hear that her or his challenging situation or condition is not condemnation from above?

A Practical Next Step

Read 2 Corinthians 12:6-10. What can we learn about healing from the apostle Paul's experience? How do we see humility in these verses? Though Paul did not receive physical healing, what do these verses indicate that Paul received from God? Now think of a time you sought healing—either physical, spiritual, mental, or emotional. How did God's response—or apparent lack of response—affect you and your view of God? Share your thoughts with God and listen for His response.

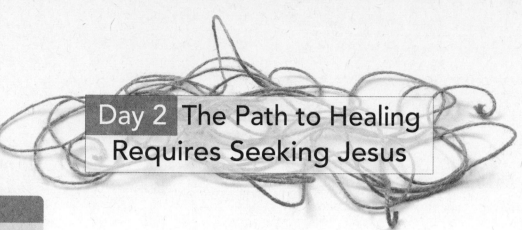

Day 2 The Path to Healing Requires Seeking Jesus

Big Idea

Healing is not a recipe to follow but a person to seek: Jesus.

Jesus's Question:
"Who touched my clothes?"
(Mark 5:30)

The Question We Ask:
Can I count on Jesus to heal me?

Leaning Into the Question

Once I was speaking at a large church in sunny Southern California for a two-day event. The first morning, I arrived hours early to set up my book table and connect with the event committee. I had started the day with a prayer I pray quite often:

Open my eyes to Your work,
Open my heart to Your will,
Open my mind to Your wisdom,
Open my life to Your way.

After the book table was set up, I headed to the coffee bar. I do love me some coffee! I had not slept well the night before and I really needed some of the brown magic liquid to help open my eyes a bit further.

There was only one other human in the coffee bar area, an attractive woman about my age. It seemed that she was focused more on the coffee than a conversation with this sleepy speaker, but when I greeted her, her demeanor changed. When we started talking, at first, we just made small talk. But then I asked her, "Are you excited about this event?"

"Not really, no." Ouch. As the speaker at this event, I did not know whether to be hurt or honored by her candor.

"Why not?" I mustered the courage to ask.

"I was widowed a few years ago and things like this bring up a lot of insecurities. I am only going to this church because my adult son loves it here and I told him if he found a church, I would go with him, but I have made no connections here, really."

Double ouch. It was not even my home church, but I could feel the heaviness of her plight.

I asked for her name (let's say it is Sarah) and promised to pray that she indeed would connect with others.

I was so struck by her willingness to be honest about her situation and seek what she needed.

We spoke for a few more minutes, then I had to make sure things were set up properly for the event. As I walked toward the sanctuary, I saw a group of ladies at a table, laughing and talking. They were a beautiful menagerie of women of all ages and cultures. I stopped in my tracks.

I went back to the coffee bar but could not find Sarah. I searched until I found her, huddled at a table by herself. "Come with me," I said.

"Where are we going?" she responded.

"Just come with me," I replied. I knew if she had an inkling about my plan, she might not follow me.

As we approached the table of ladies, I stole a chair from a neighboring table and placed it in the middle of the ladies.

I introduced myself and then explained that my good friend of seven minutes, Sarah, was looking for an amazing group of ladies with whom to hang out, and that they seemed to be the perfect candidates. They all were amiable and welcomed her to the table. I winked at her and told her I would see her later.

I did not see Sarah for the rest of the day. It is a big church and there were lots of ladies present, but I continued to pray for her to find that for which she was seeking.

The next morning at the coffee bar, I was approached from behind. I thought it was just someone trying to get their morning caffeine fix, but it was Sarah. She was smiling and jovial, and she seemed to float as she told me about the previous day. She told me how shocked she was to find out that I was the speaker, but that she had some exciting news.

"Did you know those ladies?" she asked.

"No. I do not go to this church. They just seemed awesome. Why?"

She went on to explain that the ladies at the table represented the widows' support group at the church. She told me that she did not even know that ministry existed before and that a different lady from the group has already asked to sit with her at every meal of the conference.

What an answer to my prayer (and hers)! But it might never have happened if she had not been honest about her need and begun her journey of seeking.

Leaning into the Scripture

There are a bazillion—OK, not a bazillion, but at least a hundred I can think of—examples in the Scriptures of people "seeking" in the Bible.

People with questions. People with sick children. People who were hungry. People who were at the end of their rope. People who needed a fresh start. People who were demon-possessed. People who were overcome with fear.

Many of these accounts are found in the Gospels—stories of people who were seeking Jesus. These stories inspire me to do likewise, to seek Jesus. Some of them convict me, some make me cheer and happy cry, and some do both. One such account is from Mark 5:

> 24bA large crowd followed and pressed around him. 25And a woman was there who had been subject to bleeding for twelve years. 26She had suffered a great deal under the care of many doctors and had spent all she had, yet instead of getting better she grew worse. 27When she heard about Jesus, she came up behind him in the crowd and touched his cloak, 28because she thought, "If I just touch his clothes, I will be healed." 29Immediately her bleeding stopped and she felt in her body that she was freed from her suffering.
>
> 30At once Jesus realized that power had gone out from him. He turned around in the crowd and asked, **"Who touched my clothes?"**
>
> 31"You see the people crowding against you," his disciples answered, "and yet you can ask, 'Who touched me?'"
>
> 32But Jesus kept looking around to see who had done it. 33Then the woman, knowing what had happened to her, came and fell at his feet and, trembling with fear, told him the whole truth. 34He said to her, "Daughter, your faith has healed you. Go in peace and be freed from your suffering."
>
> (Mark 5:24b-34, emphasis added)

In this story we see incredible persistence and determination. This suffering woman sought help from many doctors for years, yet she only grew worse. She had explored all the avenues she knew to get better, but to no avail. Her bleeding disorder would have kept her from the Temple (see Leviticus 15:19-33) and, no doubt, was isolating, uncomfortable, inconvenient, and stressful. It's possible that the discouragement, stress, and worry of this reality could have exacerbated her condition. There's no way to know. What we do know is that, after twelve long years with no improvement, she concluded that Jesus was her only hope. She sought to get near Him so she could touch His garment, believing that she would be healed; and she was.

Spiritual healing—the forgiveness of sins—comes before physical or other healing God might bring.

This story does not suggest that healing is like a recipe on the back of a cake box—a little bit of faith, a teaspoon of pleading, a half a cup of good fortune, and the "healing cake" comes out perfectly. Actually, sometimes healing looks like mixing the cake ingredients, baking it, and then watching as a Cornish hen comes out of the oven! The important thing to learn from this woman's example is that she sought Jesus in faith and he responded with tenderness and love, calling her "Daughter" and freeing her from her suffering.

Even when we do not receive physical healing as the woman with the bleeding disorder did, we can count on Jesus to respond to our seeking hearts with love and tenderness, granting us the inner peace and freedom we desperately need.

How do you need healing from the Lord right now? How do you relate to the woman with the bleeding disorder?

Who else in your life needs healing from the Lord? What is your prayer for him or her?

Leaning into Hope

One of the benefits of following God is healing: "Praise the Lord, my soul, and forget not all his benefits—who forgives all your sins and heals all your diseases" (Psalm 103:2-3). Note that spiritual healing—the forgiveness of sins—comes before physical or other healing God might bring. No matter what ails us, when we seek the face of God for healing, this draws us closer to Him in the process—a kind of healing in itself!

It's also important to recognize that our very salvation—our acceptance of Jesus as Savior, Lord, and risen Messiah—begins an ongoing process of healing. The Greek word *soteria*, often used for salvation, is translated "deliverance, preservation, safety, [and] salvation."[3] As we say yes to Jesus and seek to follow Him, we are walking a path of healing.

Let's end our lesson today by considering some practical ways we can press into this healing. Although this is hardly an exhaustive list, here are six *Hs* to help us remember ways we can seek healing from the Lord:

1. Humble yourself.

Allow challenges to be a time of self-examination, surrendering yourself to the Lord and the mode of healing He chooses to use, and listening for any areas of your life that are hindering your reception of healing.

> *Submit yourselves, then, to God. Resist the devil, and he will flee from you. Come near to God and he will come near to you. Wash your hands, you sinners, and purify your hearts, you double-minded. Grieve, mourn and wail. Change your laughter to mourning and your joy to gloom. Humble yourselves before the Lord, and he will lift you up.*
>
> (James 4:7-10)

2. Heed God's Word.

Read, study, and meditate on the promises of healing in the Bible. Focus on God's Word for comfort and wisdom.

> *He sent out his word and healed them;*
> *he rescued them from the grave.*
> (Psalm 107:20)

3. "Hoist" your requests to God in faith.

Trust that God can heal any spiritual, emotional, mental, or physical ailment you have.

> *"Therefore I tell you, whatever you ask for in prayer, believe that you have received it, and it will be yours."*
>
> (Mark 11:24)

4. Host a prayer session.

Ask the leaders of your church to pray for you and the affliction you are facing.

> *[14]Is anyone among you sick? Let them call the elders of the church to pray over them and anoint them with oil in the name of the Lord. [15]And the prayer offered in faith will make the sick person well; the Lord will raise them up. If they have sinned, they will be forgiven.*
>
> (James 5:14-15)

5. Have community.

Seek Jesus in community. The bleeding woman was isolated and needed to seek Jesus publicly in order to be healed. Having friends and family support and pray for you can serve to encourage you as you wait on the Lord for healing.

> *Therefore confess your sins to each other and pray for each other so that you may be healed. The prayer of a righteous person is powerful and effective.*
>
> (James 5:16)

6. Hope.

Keep praying and believing with hope; do not grow discouraged in the waiting. Continue to seek the face of God and trust in His goodness with endurance and patience!

> *¹¹Being strengthened with all power according to his glorious might so that you may have great endurance and patience, ¹²and giving joyful thanks to the Father, who has qualified you to share in the inheritance of his holy people in the kingdom of light. ¹³For he has rescued us from the dominion of darkness and brought us into the kingdom of the Son he loves, in whom we have redemption, the forgiveness of sins.*
>
> (Colossians 1:11-14)

Which of these six ways to seek the Lord for healing will you employ this week?

Was there a time when you sought Jesus for physical healing that did not come? If so, what did God reveal through that situation? What did you learn about yourself, Jesus, and your faith? What did you receive from Jesus instead?

How are you seeking Jesus for healing right now—whether physical, emotional, mental, or spiritual? How can your faith community—the body of Christ—support you on this journey to healing and wholeness?

A Practical Next Step

Write a poem about a healing challenge you are facing—whether it is emotional, mental, physical, or spiritual. Or write a letter to Jesus, describing your need for healing. How is Jesus inviting you to draw close and "touch" Him today?

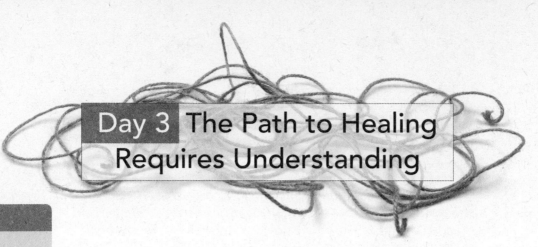

Day 3 The Path to Healing Requires Understanding

Jesus's Question:
*When Jesus looked up and saw a great crowd coming toward him,
he said to Philip, "Where shall we buy bread for these people to eat?"*
(John 6:5)

The Question We Ask:
Do I understand my deeper needs and Jesus's ability to heal them?

Leaning into the Question

As I have mentioned, I am a huge coffee fan—like "run off into the sunset" kind of affection. I have loved the stuff since I was a kid.

My mom, also an avid supporter of this caffeinated goodness, would get up very early each morning to sit on the back porch for a few hours, waking up as she consumed her morning java. Her ritual intrigued me, and when I asked if I could have some coffee too, she created a one-part coffee and twenty-parts cream-and-sugar concoction for me that began my love for a morning cup of joe. Over the years, I have reversed that to twenty-parts coffee and one-part almond creamer. I even drink it black sometimes.

So, it was an honor when our pastor called one day and asked if I would make the morning brew for the congregation. The regular (pun intended) coffee ministry person was sick, and the pastor knew I might be willing to help. He was right.

When I arrived at the church building, I was surprised to find a brewing system unlike anything I had ever used before. I kept encouraging myself by saying, "Coffee is made with three things: coffee, filter, and water (four things if you count love)." No matter how complicated the system was, I just needed to stick to coffee, filter, and water, and I would be fine—or so I thought.

I put the filter in place, did the math on how much coffee to add, and poured in enough water to fill the carafes. When the coffee started to drip, I breathed a sigh of relief.

There was a large crowd of children's ministry volunteers beginning to form, so as soon as the first batch was ready, I brought out the coffee.

No sooner had I returned to make the next batch than someone walked into the café and asked, "Who made the coffee?"

This is a trick question, right? I thought to myself. I was the only one standing there. I could not tell from the inquirer's tone of voice if the question was along the lines of "Who made this delicious coffee? It must have been kissed by Jesus Himself before it was poured into my cup" or "Who made this awful coffee? I would rather lick the floor than take another sip." Either way, I could tell that the questioner was determined to find out who had brewed the coffee.

"I made the coffee," I said. "Is there a problem?"

"Yes," he replied, "it is stone cold."

I was embarrassed and then righteously indignant. "That is impossible. I just made that pot."

"Well, it is cold."

I had to try it myself. I grabbed a Styrofoam cup from the counter and sampled the fruit of my labor. It was cold. And not the expensive cold brew kind of cold. It was cold and weak.

I went back to the coffee system to troubleshoot. Coffee, filter, water—I had all the components. That should be sufficient. But, after much investigation, I realized that behind the behemoth coffee maker was an electric cord that was not plugged in.

I had gone through the motions of making the coffee, but without a power source, the machine could only make cold, weak coffee—a travesty against humanity. Though I know how to make coffee, that day I lacked the understanding necessary to do it successfully. And as a result, I was never asked to help with the coffee ministry again!

It was not the first time nor will it be the last time that instead of being plugged in to the "power source" of God's Holy Spirit that I try and do things on my own.

Self-reliance is an amazing quality in our adult life, but the same trait in our spiritual life is not as amazing. We became aware of our need for the love of God, salvation of Christ, and the power of the Holy Spirit when we became believers, and yet, outgrowing that is not the goal—we should never outgrow our reliance upon the passion, pursuit, and power of God in our lives. Our truest, deepest need is to accept God's love, grow in our knowledge and faith, and walk in His grace and love every day.

Leaning into the Scripture

Philip, one of the followers of Jesus, had followed Jesus and seen the "formula" of love and service at work through the example of Jesus. But when it came to putting faith into practice, he still was not totally "plugged in."

Some time after this, Jesus crossed to the far shore of the Sea of Galilee (that is, the Sea of Tiberias), ²and a great crowd of people followed him because they saw the signs he had performed by healing the sick. ³Then Jesus went up on a mountainside and sat down with his disciples. ⁴The Jewish Passover Festival was near.

⁵When Jesus looked up and saw a great crowd coming toward him, he said to Philip, **"Where shall we buy bread for these people to eat?"** *⁶He asked this only to test him, for he already had in mind what he was going to do.*

⁷Philip answered him, "It would take more than half a year's wages to buy enough bread for each one to have a bite!"

(John 6:1-7, emphasis added)

Jesus asked Philip, "Where shall we buy bread for these people to eat?" (v. 5). He knew the answer, but He also knew that Philip was not totally "plugged in" to the power of God. He knew that Philip lacked full understanding of who Jesus is and what He can do.

Sadly, I can relate to Philip and his plight in this story. Sometimes I do not demonstrate full understanding of my situation or need and what Jesus can do in my life. But as I have discovered, the path to healing *requires* this kind of understanding.

During the pandemic, we watched more television than I would like to admit. One of the shows we most enjoyed is *Ted Lasso*. One of the characters on the show is named Dani Rojas, who is passionate about the game of soccer and often quoted as saying, "Football is life." It is adorable, really. He is so excited to play, especially after recovering from an injury early in the season, and his fervor for the game is contagious. This beloved character mentions having a personal faith a few times on the show, yet he is most known for saying, "Football is life."

I would say that although soccer is great, "Jesus is life," but sometimes my choices communicate otherwise.

In Lamentations 3, the prophet Jeremiah communicated His feelings about God very clearly.

²²*Because of the LORD's great love we are not consumed,*
for his compassions never fail.
²³*They are new every morning;*
great is your faithfulness.
²⁴*I say to myself, "The LORD is my portion;*
therefore I will wait for him."

²⁵The Lord is good to those whose hope is in him,
    to the one who seeks him;
²⁶it is good to wait quietly
    for the salvation of the Lord.

(Lamentations 3:22-26)

Jeremiah discovered the secret sauce to making sure his actions and choices communicate his true priorities.

"The Lord is my portion;
    therefore I will wait for him." (v. 24)

Unlike Philip, Jeremiah not only chose to make God his portion and his hope; he trusted that as he waited, God would provide everything he needed.

Speaking of portion, I love food. I think about food all the time. Even when I am not directly thinking about food, I am planning menus, researching recipes, buying groceries, checking supplies, counting calories, logging said calories, cooking, and—if I'm honest—spending energy being jealous of people who can eat a lot and stay thin.

When I am asked about my priorities, my mouth says Jesus, but my thoughts say food.

Have I asked for deliverance and healing from this? I have.

Have I asked for greater understanding of God so that I can be healed of my preoccupation with food? Once or twice—or a hundred times.

Have I become so focused on food that, like Phillip, I forget to focus on Jesus and His ability not only to meet my practical needs but also to heal my deeper needs? Affirmative.

The question Jesus asked Phillip, even though it was uttered two thousand years ago, is still important for me to ponder and answer: *where shall I buy bread to eat?* In other words, *where shall I seek to satisfy my deeper needs—to find healing for my soul?* The question reveals my need to understand my true needs and what Jesus can do in my heart and my life.

Can you relate?

Do you find yourself making things besides the Lord your portion?

Your spouse?

Your children?

Your friends?

Exercise?

Food?

Your education?

Your job?

All of these things are good. They are especially good when they are properly placed in the "Important Stuff" filing cabinet, not the "My Portion" filing cabinet.

Phillip was unsure. Phillip was confused. He let his hunger pangs grow louder than his call to follow Jesus. He let his preoccupation disallow Him from seeing the perfect plans Jesus had for him.

I have done the same thing more times than I would like to count, but I am also super thankful for God's provision as not only my Provider but also as my Portion.

What are you preoccupied with lately?

How does this preoccupation divert your focus from your deeper soul needs to more superficial needs?

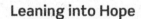

Leaning into Hope

If you can relate to the need to be healed of a lack of understanding, there is hope. Jesus is patient and asks us questions to help spur our thinking, bolster our understanding, and increase our faith.

So where can we find the true Bread of Life for our souls?

Well, even for my friends who follow a gluten-free diet, we can find some wonderful hope and practical application in some of the passages in the Gospels where Jesus talks about bread. Let's consider just a few of them.

- Jesus feeds the multitudes using fish and loaves of bread (John 6:10-13). This practical meeting of physical needs speaks to our TRUST in His goodness.
- Jesus rebukes some for following Him only for the bread—to have their fill (John 6:26-27). This candid exchange charges us to make sure our motives are pure when seeking God. It speaks to Jesus's desire for PURITY OF HEART from those who call Him Lord. Jesus instructs, "Do not work for food that spoils, but for food that endures to eternal life, which the Son of Man will give you" (John 6:27).

- Jesus reminds His followers about the bread-like substance manna that was provided to the children of Israel in the wilderness and He claims to be the Bread of Life (John 6:47-51). He is saying that He is as essential to life as the bread on tables all over the world. These verses speak about MAKING GOD OUR PORTION and trusting Him to sustain us.
- Jesus likens the Word of God to bread in His time in the desert (Matthew 4:4), proclaiming that indeed, God is our sustaining portion. This verse speaks about His desire for us to KNOW HIS WORD and follow it.
- Jesus likens the sin of the religious leaders to the leaven in bread (Matthew 16:6). This verse addresses the idea that believers should be working to LIVE A TRUE FAITH in the One who made us.
- Jesus breaks bread with his disciples at the Last Supper, the meal proceeding His death (Matthew 26:26). This action, among other things, allows us to see His heart for us to TAKE PART IN THE COMMUNITY OF CHRIST.

> Only Jesus, the Bread of Life, can heal our deeper needs.

These are just a few of the verses about bread in the Gospels that speak to us about the Bread of Life for our souls. Just as bread nourishes and sustains our bodies, giving us life, so the Bread of Life meets our deepest soul needs for nourishment and sustenance. Jesus is our life. May we grow in our trust In Him, in the purity of our hearts, in our reliance upon His provision, in our desire to know His Word, in our ability to live a true faith, and in our community with one another—all universal, deep needs of every believer. Only Jesus, the Bread of Life, can heal our deeper needs.

What are some of our universal soul needs?

What is a deeper soul need you have in this season? In other words, how is your soul in need of Jesus's healing touch? If you're unsure, perhaps the practical next step (below) will help you identify one.

How have you experienced Jesus as bread for your soul in the past? How are you hungering for bread for your soul today?

A Practical Next Step

Draw a loaf of bread on a sheet of paper and write "Jesus heals" inside it. Invite Jesus to reveal a deeper need of your soul as you spend a few minutes doodling around your drawing, allowing any images or words to surface and become part of your drawing. What do you become aware of during this creative prayer exercise?

Day 4 The Path to Healing Requires Trusting God's Heart

Jesus's Question:
"Everyone who lives and believes in Me will never die.
Do you believe this?"
(John 11:26 NASB)

The Question We Ask:
Can I trust God when healing doesn't come?

Leaning into the Question

During 2020, in the midst of the COVID-19 pandemic, one of my heroes, Florence Littauer, died. She was a pioneer in the arena of Christian Speakers and Authors, one of several who set the tone for my generation and the generations to come.

Florence was truly full of life and joy. She took great pleasure in training other speakers and authors and watching them succeed, even when they grew to surpass her in book sales and speaking fees. She and her husband often traveled together, setting an example of team ministry that my husband and I hope to replicate someday. She was a best-selling author who was quick to encourage others to write and chronicle their stories.

Florence's daughter also became a speaker and continued training others on her mother's behalf when Florence became unable to do so any longer herself.

I was so saddened to hear of her death. Though I know she is with Jesus, there was something truly remarkable about her life. I was glad that her family chose to put her service—a small gathering due to COVID—on Facebook Live so that thousands could celebrate her life, both nationally and internationally. But I am not sure anyone thought through the messaging that would be generated automatically and appear with the Facebook Live broadcast: "Click here to be notified when Florence goes live next."

At first I was mortified. She was dead. She was never "going live" again. And then I began to giggle. Of all people, Florence Littauer would have thought this hilarious. Even in her passing, she brought joy to people.

Death can seem to be the end of the story. The finale. The final inning. The period at the end of a sentence. But with God, the things we think are over are just the beginning of something new.

- Infertility (the end of the dream to bear children) can be the beginning of a journey into foster care.
- Retirement (the end of one's season of working) can mean the beginning of new freedoms and opportunities.
- Moving (the end of being in one place) can mean beginning a new chapter someplace new.
- Job loss (the end of one job) can mean beginning either a new adventure someplace new or having the freedom to find a new place to thrive, or both.
- Death (the end of one's life here on earth) means life eternal with God for those who call on the name of Jesus as Lord.

Today we are going to dive into a story where death seemed to be the end of the story. But as we will see, God can and does do amazing things even when we think the story is over.

Leaning into the Scripture

Martha, Mary, and Lazarus were siblings. They also were friends of Jesus and supporters of His ministry. They weren't just friends of Jesus—they were close friends. When Lazarus became ill, his sisters wrote to Jesus, asking him to come. But Jesus delayed, and Lazarus died.

Sometimes we can fall into thinking that if we're close to God, only good things should happen to us. But this story shows us that's just not true. Lazarus was Jesus's good friend, yet Jesus allowed him to die. Naturally, we wonder why.

Lazarus had been in the tomb for four days when Jesus arrived. It was a common belief that the soul left the body officially on day three, so day four meant the person was really dead. According to Jewish custom and common sense, Lazarus was undeniably deceased. Unlike the Egyptian custom of preparing a body for preservation through embalming, Jewish culture encouraged the decomposition of a dead body for it to return to the dust from which it came. So, upon Jesus's arrival, the body already smelled of death and despair.

Mary and Martha were clearly loved by many who came to comfort them in their time of loss. When they received word that Jesus was headed their way, Mary chose to stay with the folks in their home. Martha, on the other hand, went out to meet Him. And in her conversation with Jesus, she made some bold claims about Him:

²⁰When Martha heard that Jesus was coming, she went out to meet him, but Mary stayed at home.

²¹"Lord," Martha said to Jesus, "if you had been here, my brother would not have died. ²²But I know that even now God will give you whatever you ask."

²³Jesus said to her, "Your brother will rise again."

²⁴Martha answered, "I know he will rise again in the resurrection at the last day."

²⁵Jesus said to her, "I am the resurrection and the life. The one who believes in me will live, even though they die; ²⁶**and whoever lives by believing in me will never die. Do you believe this?**"

²⁷"Yes, Lord," she replied, "I believe that you are the Messiah, the Son of God, who is to come into the world."

(John 11:20-27)

Later, after Jesus talked with Mary and wept for his friend Lazarus, he went with the mourners to the tomb.

³⁸Jesus, once more deeply moved, came to the tomb. It was a cave with a stone laid across the entrance. ³⁹"Take away the stone," he said.

"But, Lord," said Martha, the sister of the dead man, "by this time there is a bad odor, for he has been there four days."

⁴⁰Then Jesus said, "Did I not tell you that if you believe, you will see the glory of God?"

⁴¹So they took away the stone. Then Jesus looked up and said, "Father, I thank you that you have heard me. ⁴²I knew that you always hear me, but I said this for the benefit of the people standing here, that they may believe that you sent me."

⁴³When he had said this, Jesus called in a loud voice, "Lazarus, come out!" ⁴⁴The dead man came out, his hands and feet wrapped with strips of linen, and a cloth around his face.

Jesus said to them, "Take off the grave clothes and let him go."

(John 11:38-44)

Even before Jesus miraculously raised her brother from the dead, Martha professed faith in Jesus's ability to do so. She believed who Jesus is—the Messiah, the Son of God—even when things didn't look the way she had hoped they would. She had hoped Jesus would heal Lazarus without the heartache of watching him die, burying him, and mourning his loss in the days to follow. Yet even when she didn't understand what Jesus was doing, she trusted His heart.

In this story, as in all of Jesus's miracle stories, there is manner, method, and message. Although we may not be able to understand why or how, we can trust His perfect timing, His perfect love, His perfect provision, and His perfect desire for our hearts to turn toward Him. Jesus always redeems, restores, and resurrects or brings new life—including spiritual healing wherever it is needed.

Years ago, I wrote a Bible curriculum about the miracles Jesus performed while on earth. I was so struck by the various ways that Jesus performed miracles. For example, in one instance he would use mud and spit, while in another he would heal from afar. While there is no power in the method of the miracle, it is interesting to note that the method varied according to each person and his or her need. Jesus always worked in the best interest of the patient. Here are just a few examples from a long list of miracles Jesus performed while on earth:

1. Jesus changes water into wine (John 2:1-11). Jesus meets a physical need by using water.
2. The great haul of fishes (Luke 5:1-11). After Jesus teaches a crowd, He instructs one of His followers to trust Him and place a net in the water.
3. Jesus heals a leper (Mark 1:40-45). Jesus touches the man after he begs for help.
4. Jesus stills the storm (Matthew 8:23-27). Jesus rebukes the waves with a word.
5. Jesus cures the paralytic (Matthew 9:1-8). After forgiving his sins, Jesus heals a man because of the faith of his friends.
6. Jesus loosens the tongue of a man who cannot speak (Matthew 9:32-33). Jesus heals this man both spiritually and physically.
7. Jesus heals an invalid man at the pool called Bethesda (John 5:1-9). Jesus's words alone are enough to heal this man.
8. Jesus cures a deaf and mute man (Mark 7:31-37). Jesus spits and touches the man's tongue.
9. Jesus restores the ear of the high priest's servant (Luke 22:50-51). Jesus touches the man's ear, and it is healed.
10. Jesus rises from the dead (Luke 24:5-6). God allows Jesus to die and at the proper time, raises Him from the grave.

From this list we see that God's healing work is not about the manner (the who and what) or the method (the how); it's about the message (the why). The message, or the why, is always God's heart of love and God's desire to work all things for our good.

Leaning into Hope

When we are hurting physically, mentally, emotionally, or spiritually, it can be hard to see past our hurt and need. When we have a friend or loved one who is sick and struggling, it can be difficult to see how God might use their challenges to draw them closer to Him.

But when we love through the eyes of love and in the light of eternity, we can trust that God not only can heal but also does heal people. The importance of the message is always more important than the manner or the method. And the message is always a message of love. A message that is for our good. A message that draws us closer to God.

If your heart is broken, your body is infirmed, your relationship is shattered, your faith is shaken, or your spirit is crushed, healing is truly possible by the power and grace of God. That does not mean God will heal you the way you think He should, but it does mean that you will deepen your intimacy with God as you draw close and allow Him to heal your heart and soul. You can always trust Jesus to redeem your circumstances and bring spiritual healing.

> Jesus always redeems, restores, and resurrects or brings new life—including spiritual healing wherever it is needed.

Jesus asks Martha: "Everyone who lives and believes in Me will never die. Do you believe this?" (John 11:26). Do you believe this today? Why or why not?

Are you willing to acquiesce to whatever method or manner God has in mind for your healing (or the healing of a loved one)? Explain your response.

Are you willing to trust that God has a message in either your challenge, your pain, your weakness, your illness, or all of these? Do you believe there can be redemption from your pain? How might it help you to become more like Jesus?

A Practical Next Step

Review the list of miracles (above) and circle the five that seem most miraculous to you. Why do they seem so profound? What might God be saying to you through these stories? How do they connect with your current life experience? What do you want to say to God about these observations and insights?

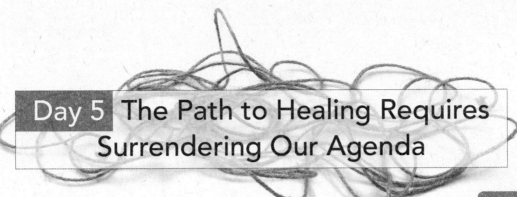

Day 5 The Path to Healing Requires Surrendering Our Agenda

Jesus's Question:
"What is your name?"
(Mark 5:9)

The Question We Ask:
Does God care about me and my need?

Leaning into the Question

My husband's older sister and her husband are practical gift people. When our son was young, in lieu of toys he didn't need, they purchased a new tool for his toolbox for each birthday and Christmas.

I remember the year that they chose to wrap his gift in racecar wrapping paper. He was in a season of car obsession—oh wait, he is still obsessed, but I digress. Convinced that the gift matched the wrapping on the outside, he prepared himself for a Hot Wheels car. But when he opened the gift, he discovered it was a wrench.

He tried to hide his disappointment, but he was not successful. Suddenly he broke into tears.

Ungrateful kid? Maybe, but I can sure relate. What about you?

During nine years of infertility, I asked for a baby, and instead I was given the strength of character that only waiting can produce.

During my father's cancer, I begged God for my dad to come to a saving knowledge of Jesus, and instead what I got was a heart for all who are lost. I asked God to heal my father's body, and instead I got a deeper friendship with my dad and reliance upon the peace of God.

During many years of limited financial resources, I asked for stuff, and instead I got a growing trust in the faithfulness of God—a much more admirable and valuable gift.

Now that he is older, our son realizes that the toys of his childhood have all broken, been donated, or were handed down to younger cousins. But those tools? Well, they have been invaluable as he has had to fix things on his car or work on other projects. His aunt and uncle had the foresight to provide the best gift even before Josiah knew how perfect those tools would become.

Sometimes, that is how healing from God works. Does it always look like we think it might? No. Do we understand or appreciate the type of healing He provides at the time it happens? Rarely. Is it what is best for us because He loves us? Yes, even when we throw a fit because we think we know best.

Leaning into the Scripture

As a child, I disliked having an unusual name. I could never find a mug at a truck stop with my name on it. People misspelled it, mispronounced it, and made fun of it. So, for much of my childhood, I wanted a different name. Jennifer. Elizabeth. Michelle. Soybean. Anything other than Amberly. Amberly was unusual. Amberly was often mispronounced. Amberly stood out, and I did not want to do that. My agenda was to have a more common name.

My mom named me after a morally questionable character in an old romance novel. This character, Amber, may have been beautiful, confident, and well versed in using her feminine wiles for her gain, but I was none of those things. I just wanted to fit in. But my name disallowed me to be common or ordinary—well, my name *and* my volume!

When I was ten years old, a friend invited me to church, and I went. It was there that I truly felt God call me to Himself. I chose to be baptized, and I felt so understood, so cherished by God. But at my baptism, the man performing the ritual had trouble with my name, saying, "Ammmmmberly."

He wasn't alone. When I graduated from high school, the announcer said—instead of Amberly Eproson—Kimberly Erosion (no kidding!). In college, after changing my surname to Neese, everyone said my first name correctly but pronounced my last name Neesey. Was it so much to want someone to say my name correctly? In all these instances, a person asked me my name, but most did not carefully listen for the answer.

Most people get names wrong because they are not listening. I have heard that we have a hard time remembering other people's names because we are listening for them to say our name correctly. Ouch.

I am guilty of this for sure. I will be sad if we do not have nametags (or an automatic mental download of everyone's name) in heaven, because I am the worst at names. I totally need to work on my listening skills!

Jesus, on the other hand, is a great listener. He truly hears people—their names, their needs, and their hearts. But Jesus not only listens when He asks people questions; maybe equally important, He asks questions so the person has a chance to process internally.

Mark 5 chronicles a story of Jesus and the disciples crossing the lake to the region of the Gerasenes. As Jesus was leaving the boat in which they were traveling,

a man with what the Bible calls an "impure spirit" left one of the tombs in which he lived and came toward Jesus. It was said this man was so out of control that he would cut himself with stones and cry out night and day; and that no one could bind and subdue him, not even with a chain.

The man ran and fell on his knees in front of Jesus when he saw Him from a distance. When Jesus was trying to rid the man of the impure spirit, he raised his voice and shouted loudly, "What do you want with me, Jesus, Son of the Most High God? In God's name don't torture me!" (Mark 5:7). Clearly, it wasn't the man speaking but the demons within him.

Even though Jesus knew the answer, He asked: **"What is your name?"** (Mark 5:9, emphasis added).

The man answered that his name was Legion because of the number of demons inside him, and begged Jesus not to expel them out of the area.

Why would the name of the demons matter? Why would Jesus ask such a question?

The story in Mark 5 continues:

> [14]*Those tending the pigs ran off and reported this in the town and countryside, and the people went out to see what had happened.* [15]*When they came to Jesus, they saw the man who had been possessed by the legion of demons, sitting there, dressed and in his right mind; and they were afraid.* [16]*Those who had seen it told the people what had happened to the demon-possessed man—and told about the pigs as well.* [17]*Then the people began to plead with Jesus to leave their region.*
>
> [18]*As Jesus was getting into the boat, the man who had been demon-possessed begged to go with him.* [19]*Jesus did not let him, but said, "Go home to your own people and tell them how much the Lord has done for you, and how he has had mercy on you."* [20]*So, the man went away and began to tell in the Decapolis how much Jesus had done for him. And all the people were amazed.*
>
> (Mark 5:14-20)

The people in the area went from being afraid, to wanting Jesus to leave the region, to being amazed.

What was the man like before meeting Jesus? After meeting Jesus?

What were you like before you met Jesus? How have you changed since then?

Jesus instructed the man to "tell (others) how much the Lord has done" for him. List five things that the Lord has done for you since you came to faith in Him.

1.

2.

3.

4.

5.

Leaning into Hope

I find it interesting that after Jesus rid the man of the impure spirits and placed them into a herd of pigs, we never learn the man's real name—not the moniker given to him by the evil spirits, but the name designating who he truly was. As the Son of God, Jesus knew this man's real name and his need. And He shined light on that need for deliverance and healing through His question to the demon-possessed man.

Jesus knows the questions to ask to get to the heart of our needs too, because He sees us and loves us deeply. This gives us hope because sometimes putting a name on our issue facilitates our healing. Sometimes identifying and labeling a sin or a wrong or an ailment or a stressor can relieve some of its power.

You may feel like you have a legion of issues, regrets, weaknesses, wounds, and sin patterns. But just as Jesus freed the demon-possessed man, He wants to free you and me from the bondage of all that holds us captive. No matter the challenge, Jesus is able to rid us of whatever is wielding power over us.

The man possessed by demons may not have his name recorded in the Bible, but he is known and loved by God. His story is an example of the miraculous healing power of God in Jesus—power that gives hope to all who are struggling.

God knows your name, and He knows what you are facing. Look to Him and find your hope and healing, even if it does not look like you think it should.

A name is personal. Even those who have a common name have a personal connection to their bestowed moniker. The fact that Jesus knows our name makes it personal. But it is not just our name that He knows—He knows us. And He loves us and cares for us enough to call us by name.

In addition to knowing our name, Jesus is familiar with our needs. One of those needs is our need for Him to help us lay down our own agendas—which are not always helpful—so that He may work in us and for us.

You see, Jesus is always for us, even when things don't look as we might want them to—when our checking accounts don't look like we think they should, when our relationships do not look like we think they should, and when our healing does not look like we think it should.

> Jesus is always for us, even when things don't look as we might want them to.

He loves us enough to draw us close to Him, allowing us to hear His heart beat for us and teaching us to trust that His ways are better than ours.

My friend, God sees you and your need and wants to set you free from all that holds you captive!

When have you had to surrender your agenda or expectations on the path to healing? What did that look like or involve?

How has Jesus demonstrated in the past that He sees you and your need? How have you seen the power of God at work in areas where you have been held captive?

How does this story in Mark 5 encourage you in a current struggle?

A Practical Next Step

Make a list of the ways that God's healing work has been and is now evident in your life.

Then take a few moments and praise God for His healing power in your life—past, present, and future.

How did this exercise encourage you for any healing (your own or that of others) that you still may be waiting on?

Week 4 | Wrap-up

Prayer was a difficult topic to tackle last week, but I think healing is an even grander labyrinth to navigate, no matter our spiritual background and journey.

I hate taking out the trash. It is my least favorite household chore. When I was younger, my sister and I had chores that rotated, and I would consistently bargain with her to do the dishes rather than collect and dispose of the trash. She always obliged, maybe because she is a great sister, or maybe because trash took six minutes to complete while dishes took twenty.

When people talk about dumpster diving, I am intrigued, but from a distance. It truly grosses me out. Once, while working at a Christian camp, a camper misplaced his retainer, so a few staff members and I climbed into the giant trash receptacle to help him locate the orthodontia. I know Jesus said, "Greater love has no one than this, that a person will lay down his life for his friends" (John 15:13 NASB), but I felt, at that moment, that standing in that trash bin, sorting through discarded food, napkins, packaging, and overall yuck, was as close I had come to the kind of love about which Jesus spoke.

I didn't lay down my life in search of the retainer, I just laid down my pride, my comfort, and my ability to smell good.

When the topic of healing comes up, we as believers are eternally grateful for the fact that Jesus did indeed "lay down His life for His friends [you and me]." Accepting this truth and the fact that Jesus is the risen Lord is the ultimate healing.

But what about other types of healing? As we have discussed this week, healing is a complicated issue. Some of what people have purported to be true is a bunch of trash—namely, that healing is based on righteousness, is only for believers, is limited to physical healing, or is a guarantee. The questions of Jesus we explored this week helped us dispel the trash from the treasure, so we may hold on to the treasure related to healing—which includes practicing humility, seeking Jesus, understanding our deeper needs, trusting God's heart, and surrendering our agenda. Let's hold on to this treasure as we continue navigating the path to healing and wholeness.

> "Greater love has no one than this, that a person will lay down his life for his friends" (John 15:13 NASB).

Of the questions we've explored, which one resonates most, and why?

What questions do you still have related to healing?

Read the week's memory verse, Psalm 103:2-4, slowly several times. Is there a word or phrase that catches your attention or touches your heart? What does God have to say to you about the word or phrase in light of your current life experience? How is God inviting you to respond?

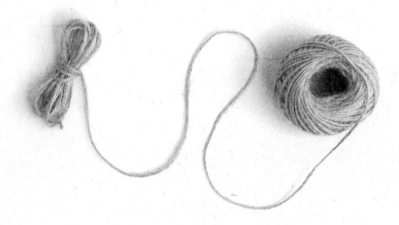

Video Viewer Guide Week 4

What Must I Do to Be Healed?

Memory Verse:

Psalm 103:2-4 NIV

Revere:

_____ the LORD, my soul,

_____ is remembering who He is

Recall:

...and _____ _____ all his benefits—

Restored:

...who _____ all your sins

and _____ all your diseases,

Redeemed:

...who _____ your life from the pit

Receive:

...and _____ you with love and compassion.

Permission Slip:

This week, we tackled the concept of healing—a multifaceted issue indeed. We unearthed some of the misnomers of healing and some of the keys to it—practicing humility, seeking Jesus, understanding our deeper needs, trusting God's heart, and surrendering our agenda.

You have permission to _____.

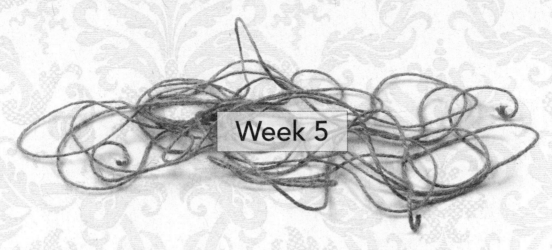

What Is God's Plan for Us?

MEMORY VERSE:

Show me your ways, Lord,
teach me your paths.
Guide me in your truth and teach me,
for you are God my Savior,
and my hope is in you all day long.

(Psalm 25:4-5)

In our house, frugality is an art form, a well-honed skill trained from birth. We joke that it was or was not God's will for us to have a particular item depending on whether it was in the sale flyer from the grocery store.

That is a silly overgeneralization of a very complex idea.

The will of God has been something Bible scholars and sojourners alike have discussed, studied, and discerned for ages. It has been the topic of much debate and is the basis for denominational splits, especially when coupled with free will.

We are not going to dive into the debates this week, but we are going to examine some of the irrefutable truths about what God wants for all of His people.

Are you unsure if you know the will of God for your life? Are you unsure you can even know it?

You are not alone, friend. Even folks in the Bible struggled with discerning such things.

Gideon was more than the name on the Bibles in hotel rooms across the nation. He was a military leader, prophet, and judge in Israel. When the Israelites were in trouble in a battle against the Midianites, God asked Gideon to help lead His people to victory. God called him a mighty warrior (Judges 6:12), but Gideon was not so sure.

Gideon eschewed God's call. He was wrestling with his faith, wondering why such trouble would befall the people of God if God was on their side. He felt God had, on some level, abandoned His people, yet Gideon cried out for grace.

God was indeed graceful, and despite Gideon's doubt and uncertainty of God's will and plans, God used Gideon in mighty ways to lead His people.

Like Gideon, we have doubts and often wrestle with questions, but God wants to use each of us in mighty ways. Knowing some universal truths about God's plans for His people can help us to yield our lives—and our wills—to His.

Day 1 God's Plan for Us Is to Have Enduring Faith

Jesus's Question:
"Why did you doubt?"
(Matthew 14:26)

The Question We Ask:
Where is God when life is hard?

Leaning into the Question

I love a good movie. I also love consuming fourteen buckets of buttered popcorn in the theater while enjoying a good flick, but that is another story.

In the great movie series *Back to the Future*, there are many memorable characters. The protagonist, Marty McFly, is played by the unforgettable Michael J. Fox, the sweetheart of television who, although he had made another movie prior to this one, made his mark in the film industry as the lead in this movie. Dr. Emmett Brown, played skillfully by the goofy and very funny Christopher Lloyd, is Marty's friend and somewhat mad scientist, who discovers the secret to time travel and drags Marty into the ensuing chaos.

The one character I have trouble connecting with in this film is Marty's father, George McFly. He is bumbling, insecure, bullied, timid, and pathetic. Years of verbal and physical abuse from a classmate-turned-boss have depleted him of confidence, backbone, and strength. I find the scenes with him painful because of the depth of his hurt. His character is so uncomfortable, in fact, that I want the movie to fast-forward to when he finds his confidence and becomes a new man (sorry, spoiler from a movie released thirty-six years ago!).

But growth does not work that way. Nor does faith. We do not have the luxury of fast-forwarding through the process of learning, struggling, stretching, making mistakes, and getting stronger.

Had I fast-forwarded through the story of George McFly, I would have missed the humor and great storytelling of the whole movie. I would have missed the heart.

When we face difficulty, even the most lion-hearted among us sometimes wish to fast-forward through the discomfort, pain, challenge, uncertainty, frustration, and unknown. But if we had the power to travel through time and skip the unfun parts of life, we also would miss the lessons therein. We wouldn't become stronger, more resilient, more tenacious, more patient, and more persistent in our faith. And thankfully, God loves us too much to allow us to miss those faith-building lessons. Though God doesn't cause challenges to teach us lessons, He does redeem them for our good and our growth. God doesn't cause storms but uses them to strengthen our faith.

Leaning into the Scripture

Right after Jesus feeds thousands (and by the way, this is one of my favorite miracles of Jesus; any time there is food involved, you have my attention!), He and His disciples immediately get into a boat. I guess the old warning not to go into the water for thirty minutes after you eat doesn't apply when you are with the Savior, right? But as we will see, one of them in the boat is definitely going for a swim! In Matthew's account we read:

> *22Immediately Jesus made the disciples get into the boat and go on ahead of him to the other side, while he dismissed the crowd. 23After he had dismissed them, he went up on a mountainside by himself to pray. Later that night, he was there alone, 24and the boat was already a considerable distance from land, buffeted by the waves because the wind was against it.*
>
> *25Shortly before dawn Jesus went out to them, walking on the lake. 26When the disciples saw him walking on the lake, they were terrified. "It's a ghost," they said, and cried out in fear.*
>
> *27But Jesus immediately said to them: "Take courage! It is I. Don't be afraid."*
>
> *28"Lord, if it's you," Peter replied, "tell me to come to you on the water."*
>
> *29"Come," he said.*
>
> *Then Peter got down out of the boat, walked on the water and came toward Jesus. 30But when he saw the wind, he was afraid and, beginning to sink, cried out, "Lord, save me!"*
>
> *31Immediately Jesus reached out his hand and caught him. "You of little faith," he said, "why did you doubt?"*
>
> *32And when they climbed into the boat, the wind died down. 33Then those who were in the boat worshiped him, saying, "Truly you are the Son of God."*
>
> (Matthew 14:22-33)

In this passage Jesus asks a question that pertains not only to Peter but also to all His followers.

There was a boat full of apostles that day (I picture them much like George McFly at times!), yet Peter was the only one who chose to get out of the boat.

Jesus's question is directed to believers who are too afraid to venture out in faith as well as to those who follow God with fervor and then become fearful when the waves (or storms) of life come.

The apostles were privy to the amazing things Jesus did on a daily basis, yet they doubted. They had just seen Him exchange a boy's lunch for a feast for thousands, but they did not have the courage or the faith to trust that He could sustain them in the storm. They could not see past their doubt when it came to seeing Jesus for who He is and what He can do. They chose not to remember all He had done and step out in faith accordingly.

There are a few words for "remember" in Hebrew, the language of the Old Testament. One such verb is *zakar*.[1] However in Jewish tradition, the concept of remembrance involves more than just recalling something, as one might do with an actor's name or a phone number. Remembrance implies awareness as well as taking some sort of action on behalf of the person or thing that is being remembered.

When we struggle with trust, one of the most powerful choices we can make includes recalling the good God has done and then acting accordingly. Walking in the truth of His goodness can help us walk in our present struggles, even when (and sometimes especially when) the storms of life seem overwhelming.

We discussed God's faithfulness in Week 2, but it is worth revisiting because when the storms of life come, our experiences and recollections of the faithfulness of God can serve as lifeboats in the storms of life.

When we struggle to trust, these recollections can shape our choices and behaviors and help the winds seem smaller as God becomes bigger in our vision.

> When we struggle with trust, one of the most powerful choices we can make includes recalling the good God has done and then acting accordingly.

What is the greatest thing in your recollection that can be attributed to God?

If you were one of the apostles, which of Jesus's miraculous acts would seem the most remarkable to you? Why?

How often do you take the time to recall the works of God? Do your everyday actions reflect your trust in God? Why or why not?

Leaning into Hope

Peter had great intentions. He wanted to be like Jesus and walk on the water.

We all have had spurts of incredible clarity and faith when our faith has been chugging along on all cylinders. We have all taken steps toward Jesus as Peter did.

But when Peter took His eyes off Jesus and "saw the wind," he began to sink (v. 30). It must have been pretty epic wind if Peter saw it, not just felt it. It must have seemed scary. Even with Jesus in his purview, Peter chose to give more gravity to the wind than to the words and encouragement of Jesus.

Storms happen in our lives all the time. Though the winds of difficulty in your life might look different from mine, any winds can certainly take our eyes off Jesus if we let them.

Handling the loss of a job. Mourning the death of someone you love. Navigating divorce. Functioning through an inability to sleep well. Shouldering financial obligations. Orchestrating relocation. Battling chronic illness. Sorting through interpersonal conflict. Maneuvering injury. Working through emotional problems (depression, anxiety, anger, guilt, and low self-esteem, to name a few). Choosing to care for a family member who is elderly or sick. Dealing with a traumatic event, such as a natural disaster, theft, rape, or violence against you or a loved one.

Even happy events can feel like wind.

Getting married. Having a baby. Watching your "babies" grow up and leave home. Having grandchildren. Getting a promotion at work. Making a new friend.

Throughout it all, God wants to us to trust Him through the winds of challenge. The winds of change. The winds of uncertainty. God promises to strengthen our faith through the storms of life.

What winds are you facing right now?

What would need to be different for you to focus only on the words and encouragement of Jesus?

A Practical Next Step

Connect with someone this week whose faith has endured and grown through difficult times. Ask them about the things God has done in their life and how it has shaped their faith.

Day 2 God's Plan for Us Is to Have a Hope and a Future

Jesus's Question:
*"Are you not in error because you do not know
the Scriptures or the power of God?"*
(Mark 12:24)

The Question We Ask:
Is God going to come through for me?

Leaning into the Question

When our kids were little and they would get hungry (which seemed like every 2.47 seconds!), I often found myself answering their cries of "starvation" with questions: *Have you ever gone without food? Have I ever forgotten to feed you? Do you know that you are loved?* Although these questions seem innocuous, I often asked the questions with equal parts sarcasm and frustration. Although I never verbalized it to my kids, my mental ticker tape read something like: *Do I look like a vending machine? Do you not know how much I have to get done today? Do you know how blessed you are that you are cute?* But I also knew that it was a season.

The season you are in may be a difficult one indeed, or things may be downright easy-breezy-beautiful for you right now, but remember, it is called a season for a reason (my poetry is inspiring, isn't it?). However it is, it will not last—things will change, relationships will evolve, you will age, you will get stronger, you will develop perseverance, you will grow, and you will be tested.

I think it so interesting that the word *season* means both "a time characterized by a particular circumstance or feature" and "to give (food) more flavor or zest."[2] God desires for us to live a life of purpose, flavor, and abundance; and He uses the difficult seasons of our lives, as well as the delightful ones, to mold us, shape us, and make us stronger.

My favorite cut of meat or roasting vegetables do not have a choice regarding whether or not they will endure seasoning when in my kitchen, but you and I can choose every day to trust that when God is "seasoning" us, it is for our benefit and His glory.

My son and I are taking a pump class two days a week at our gym. It involves all sorts of equipment, including a myriad of weights and bands. Most days, after the class is over, I feel like a T. rex—not because I am strong and powerful, but because I cannot lift my arms and they hang useless at my side. But I am getting stronger. I am able to handle heavier weights for longer periods of time. Why? Because of practice. The time I have spent struggling, panting, cursing (to myself, of course), and sweating are starting to pay off.

Oftentimes, we resent seasons of difficulty, not choosing to see how they have made us into the stronger people we are today because of the heavy lifting done in that season. Rarely do we look back in gratitude over the days, months, and years that have shaped us into who we are because of those hard days.

Because I signed up for and pay to take the pump class with my son, I'm choosing to submit myself to the resistance. I guess you could say I've asked for the pain, right? I choose twice a week to endure this difficulty because I can see the muscles I am developing after those two difficult hours in my week. Sometimes pushing through the class makes me feel downright brave. Maybe you can relate when it comes to some of the difficulties you are facing right now.

Recently, I asked on my social media for people to share the bravest thing they had done. Some gave funny (and honest!) answers like "have kids," while others shared major feats of bravery:

- leaving an abusive marriage,
- fostering kids,
- going to therapy,
- chasing robbers out of the garage,
- quitting a toxic job,
- flying internationally as a child by myself,
- moving across country,
- leaving home, and
- wearing a wire for the police to get a confession from my son.

Wow. Those are brave decisions, many of which were made in really tough seasons. These folks did not sign up for these difficulties, yet they have been changed by their willingness to be brave and come out stronger.

Jeremiah 29:11 is one of the most quoted verses in the Bible:

"For I know the plans I have for you," declares the Lord, "plans to prosper you and not to harm you, plans to give you hope and a future."

I have seen it posted on a million graduation cards, but rarely do people address the context in which it was said.

The prophet Jeremiah was addressing the Israelites whose ancestors had been oppressed by both the Egyptian and Babylonian empires (enemies of the Jewish people), had been exiled from Jerusalem to Babylon (having to leave their homeland and go to a foreign country), and had been dealing with incredible disappointment. They had been misled by the prophet Hananiah, who had told them that God would save them by breaking the yoke of oppression, freeing them, and allowing them to return to their homeland within two years, which undoubtedly gave them false hope. Jeremiah, on the other hand, rebuked Hananiah (Jeremiah 28:15-17) and provided a reality check for the people of Israel, saying that they not only would be in exile for at least seventy years but also should establish themselves there by marrying, praying for peace in Babylon, and settling down (Jeremiah 29:4-10).

This is not a greeting card verse as we often use it! It is being spoken over a group of faithful folks who understood suffering, were in need of rescue, and desired an immediate solution. Instead of a quick fix, this verse is designed to encourage them that despite their current distress and difficulty, God still has plans to give them a future full of promise and hope.

We can be comforted by this verse because we too are not promised a quick fix, a rescue that looks like we think it should, a "get out of jail free" card for suffering and hardship. Instead, we have a promise from God to work for our good.

As Christians facing difficult situations today, we can take comfort in Jeremiah 29:11, knowing that it is not a promise of immediate rescue from hardship or suffering but a promise that God has a plan for our lives; regardless of our current situation, He can work through it to prosper us and give us a hope and a future.

Take another look at this part of the verse:

*"For **I know** the plans I have for you," declares the Lord (emphasis added).*

God knows the plans He has for us. Nowhere in this verse has He promised a GPS overview of all His plans for us. He does not promise *we* will know the plans He has for us. But He does promise hope and intentionality. He does not promise that *our* plans will give us a hope and a future, but that *His* will.

Jesus tried to redirect His followers to the plans of God with regard to His own life, as we see in Mark 12.

Leaning into the Scripture

Midway in chapter 12 of Mark's Gospel we see Jesus facing a group of Sadducees and standing in a trap they have set for him. Sadducees were members "of a Jewish sect or party of the time of Christ that denied the resurrection of the dead, the existence of spirits, and the obligation of oral tradition, emphasizing acceptance of the written Law alone."[3]

One of my Bible teachers in college used to remind us that the Sadducees had no hope in the afterlife, so they were "sad, you see." They were not convinced that there was "hope and a future" for them after they died, and they wanted to trap Jesus with questions about the afterlife:

> [18]*Then the Sadducees, who say there is no resurrection, came to him with a question.* [19]*"Teacher," they said, "Moses wrote for us that if a man's brother dies and leaves a wife but no children, the man must marry the widow and raise up offspring for his brother.* [20]*Now there were seven brothers. The first one married and died without leaving any children.* [21]*The second one married the widow, but he also died, leaving no child. It was the same with the third.* [22]*In fact, none of the seven left any children. Last of all, the woman died too.* [23]*At the resurrection whose wife will she be, since the seven were married to her?"*

> [24]*Jesus replied,* ***"Are you not in error because you do not know the Scriptures or the power of God?"***
>
> (Mark 12:18-24, emphasis added)

The Sadducees are playing a verbal and theological chess game with Jesus, thinking that with enough strategy and cunning they can trap Him into saying something blasphemous—something that would contradict God's Word and make Him a guilty party. They themselves do not even believe in the idea of resurrection, yet they ask questions about it. They intertwine their knowledge of the law of Moses (the first five books of the Old Testament, called the Pentateuch) with their desire to catch Jesus in a misspoken word.

The Sadducees are so familiar with the Scriptures of the Old Testament that they pridefully preface their question with "Moses wrote for us" (v. 19, emphasis added). Their words communicate that God wrote through Moses for all the Jews, but in light of their pride in their dealings with Jesus and others in their society, I wonder if their hearts were more focused on themselves. Perhaps their place in society had fanned the flame of their pride. Author Mike Nappa says that "they were known as much for their wealth and corruption as for their religious devotion."[4]

More About the Sadducees[5]

1. They were called a "brood of vipers" by John the Baptist (Matthew 3:7).
2. They were powerful and wealthy.
3. They were dedicated to the Temple and held power and control over it, as well as the Sanhedrin—the governing body for both religious and legal issues between Jews.
4. They opposed the Pharisees but sat with them as members of the Sanhedrin.
5. They followed the laws of Moses for financial gain and job security in the Sanhedrin, not out of religious zeal.
6. They oversaw Temple worship and often held the role of high priest or chief priest.
7. They did not believe in the supernatural—angels, heaven, hell, or resurrection.
8. They asserted that God did not play an active role in everyday life.
9. They were likely involved in the plot to arrest and crucify Jesus.
10. The Sadducees were part of the highest class in Judean society, but not because of their commitment to God. We might say they were religious rock stars but faith failures. Though it is easy for us to judge these religious leaders for their shortsightedness and shortcomings, sometimes we have an "inner Sadducee" within us—a part of us that is more concerned about appearances than true devotion to God.

Jesus knew the Sadducees were trying to trap him. He knew they were not searching for answers but were seeking to affirm their own beliefs. So He asked them, "Isn't this the reason you are wrong, because you don't know either the scriptures or God's power?" (Mark 12:24 CEB).

With this question, Jesus hits them where it counts—in their religiosity. In their desire to be right, he proclaims them wrong. In their desire to look wise, He calls out their ignorance of the Scriptures as well as their lack of relationship to God. Ouch.

When I read Jesus's question in Mark 12:24, I read it with a sarcastic tone. Some people believe that sarcasm is neither effective nor efficient communication. Some even find it inappropriate. But for me, sarcasm is my third language, after English and food. I believe sarcasm can be an effective tool in my communication toolbox when used with care and precision, as I imagine Jesus might have used it here.

No matter how we read Jesus's question, we can be sure He is not messing around! He is warning the apostles of the evil of those seeking to kill Him. Jesus is not afraid of dying, but He wants His followers to recognize the gravity of the season they are in and the cost of following Him.

Do the words of Jeremiah 29:11 pertain to Jesus and His followers? You bet they do! The cross may not seem like "hope and a future" for Jesus, but God sent His Son to earth so that you and I would have hope and a future, and so that He would be glorified in it all. God was working His good will in the life of Jesus, just as He works His good will in the lives of those who follow Him.

God desires to give hope and a future to all His children. We can be assured of this fact through God's promises (His Word), God's passion (His heart), and God's power (His deeds).

Though Jesus is addressing the Sadducees here in Mark 12, his question gets to the heart of our doubt when we are uncertain because things aren't going the way we planned. The question for each of us might be "Am I doubting that God will come through for me—that God is working for my good—because I'm forgetting God's promises, God's passion, and God's power?"

When we doubt, often our problem is that we are either unfamiliar with or unmindful of God's promises, passion, and power—in the Bible and in our own lives.

To which characteristic of the Sadducees do you most relate, and why?

How would someone know that you trust God's promises, passion, and power? What is the evidence for this in your life?

When has a difficult circumstance caused you to doubt or question God's ability to work things for your good? What happened?

Leaning into Hope

The more time we spend studying and applying the promises in God's Word, seeking the passion (or heart) of God through the Word and through prayer, and reminding ourselves and those around us of the power of God, the more we will trust God's plans with courage and strength in the midst of challenges.

> When we struggle with trust, one of the most powerful choices we can make includes recalling the good God has done and then acting accordingly.

The Sadducees knew the Septuagint, the Greek Old Testament, but they focused primarily on the laws. They seemed to disallow any of their knowledge of God to affect their daily lives.

Knowing stuff about God and actually knowing Him are two different things. The Sadducees knew a lot about God, but they did not really know His love, His redemptive power, or His plans.

Jesus's question must have stung the Sadducees. These men had spent much of their lives learning the Scriptures, but they focused mostly on the rituals of the Temple. The Bible was only a reference of knowledge for them, not a source of transformation. They knew the Word of God but not the heart of God. They knew the rules of God but failed to seek a relationship with God. They relied on the power of religiosity rather than a relationship with the God of the universe.

We may judge the Sadducees, but oftentimes we practice similar habits. We might know scripture without seeking to discover and live its truth. We might pray without inviting God into our everyday lives and allowing Him to transform us.

Today God is inviting us to trust Him by focusing our minds and hearts on His Word, His heart, and His deeds—both in scripture and in our own lives. When we place our confidence in God's promises, passion, and power, we increase our confidence in the truth that God is always working to give us hope and a future!

What makes it difficult for you to place your confidence in God's promises (His Word), God's passion (His heart), and God's power (His deeds in the Bible and our own lives)? Which of these three *Ps* is most challenging for you to trust, and why?

How are you putting this week's Memory Verse into practice? As we've learned from the Sadducees, true faith is not only knowing or memorizing truth but also actualizing it in our lives.

Show me your ways, Lord,
teach me your paths.
Guide me in your truth and teach me,
for you are God my Savior,
and my hope is in you all day long.
(Psalm 25:4-5)

How are you noticing God's ways (or deeds, actions) each day?

How are you allowing God to teach you each day?

How are you placing your hope in God each day?

A Practical Next Step

Spend ten minutes in prayer, talking with God about your struggles, hopes, and dreams. Be completely raw and real, holding nothing back. Then invite God to bring to your mind examples of His promises, passion, and power—from His Word and from your own life. Sit with these and "rehearse" them in your mind. How is God inviting you to believe in His promise of hope and a future for your life?

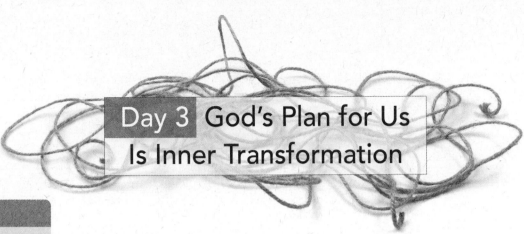

Day 3 God's Plan for Us Is Inner Transformation

Jesus's Question:

"Why do you entertain evil thoughts in your hearts?
Which is easier: to say, 'Your sins are forgiven,'
or to say, 'Get up and walk'?"
(Matthew 9:4-5)

The Question We Ask:

If God knows my secret thoughts, is He angry with me?

Leaning into the Question

We were visiting our local zoo recently. This zoo contains many of the indigenous animals of the desert and allows many of these critters to roam free throughout the campus. As we walked, we encountered peacocks, roadrunners, and a six-foot snake. He wasn't interested in any of us, but that did not stop my heart from doing jumping jacks.

I could read random animal facts all day. Animals are fascinating indeed, but mostly, God's wisdom in the creation and protection of animals is so amazing. He crafted each with strengths and weaknesses, beauty, and survival.

We made our way through the zoo, stopping at each enclosure, hoping to get a good glimpse of the animals housed inside. When we got to the eagle's aviary, I was transfixed. The birds are so majestic, so regal, so beautiful. I must have taken 834 photos on my phone, but none could capture its plumage, coloring, or demeanor. We were admiring this creature with at least ten other people when something amazing happened—the snake we had seen earlier actually slithered into the eagle's cage. We all took a collective breath. This group of zoo visitors who had been chatting and admiring the bird just moments before suddenly became mimes. We all fell silent. Why? We wanted to watch this gloriously feathered beast attack that snake. We thought for sure we were about to watch an episode of a TV show from Animal Planet or *Mutual of Omaha's Wild Kingdom* (if you're close to my age, you know!).

The snake moved throughout the cage with no regard for the massive predator perched above him. At first, I thought the bird did not see the snake. But according to the placard in front of the cage, its vision is four to eight times stronger than that of a human.

The zoo visitors began to grow restless. After sitting in silence for about three minutes, one of the men in the group said, "C'mon! Get him! Eat that snake! He will be delicious!"

The eagle was impervious to the man's coaxing. The bird just perched on his pedestal, ignoring the others who began to egg him on (no pun intended). The snake continued to move freely throughout the cage, unaware that the onlooking humans were hoping for its demise. Soon, people grew restless once they accepted the fact that the eagle was not interested in a feast of a snake and moved on to the next cage.

I will admit, I was hoping for a smackdown in the animal kingdom that day. I had my camera ready to capture the cage fight, but to no avail. We thought for sure we knew the ending of the story, but we were mistaken.

I am so glad my inner thoughts were not broadcast at the zoo. They would have borne witness to a church lady yelling at a bird to commit heinous violence against one of God's creatures . . . in Jesus's name, of course.

Every family has its culture of what is acceptable or not. In our family, we never wanted our kids to say something in public that would embarrass our ancestors, so we did not teach them restroom words that we would be uncomfortable for them to say aloud in the grocery store.

Friends of ours took a different approach. They were tired of the negative talk so prevalent in society, so they taught their kids that there were three non-cuss words that were off limits: stupid, hate, and kill. There were penalties for using these words in their home and most often, it worked beautifully for them.

Until one day, in anger, one of the kids said all three words together. Mom overheard the exchange and confronted the young man about what he had said. He was honest about it and took full responsibility, but he still cried when Mom asked him to go to his room and think about what he had done.

When she went to check on him a few minutes later, she was shocked. He was sitting at the edge of the bed softly repeating, "Stupid, hate, kill, stupid, hate, kill, stupid hate, kill . . ."

"What are you doing?" she asked.

"You told me to sit on my bed and think about what I had done. I am thinking about it," he responded.

His innocence made her smile.

"I meant that I wanted you to think about other things you could have said, but I am thankful that you have given your actions and words proper thought."

After that, in private, the parents would often laugh about the incident. They admit that when they get *really* mad, instead of a curse word, they just say "Stupid, hate, kill." It not only diffuses their anger, it also serves as a reminder of the candor of a child.

Just as the words we say can be damaging, so our inner dialogue can be destructive and corrosive as well. Jesus knows our thoughts—yet loves us and offers us forgiveness. But these religious leaders, instead of seeking forgiveness, were threatened by Him. Instead of rejoicing over the healing of a man, they were indignant (inner dialogue) about Jesus healing him spiritually by forgiving his sins.

Sometimes, we too can miss the point when it comes to the works of God, especially when it comes to our inner dialogue. My inner dialogue is often the place where the truest level of my faith in God is clear.

I can help an elderly person by opening the door and smiling, but my inner dialogue might be saying, "Hurry up, lady! C'mon!"

I can put on a facade of confidence and self-kindness, but my inner dialogue often is hypercritical of every extra pound, wrinkle, and imperfection.

When our car breaks down and the bill is thousands of dollars, I am quick to tell the mechanic through a smile that "God will provide," yet my inner dialogue screams, "Are you kidding me, God! This is the fifth financial blow this month!"

God wants us to trust Him with both our outer and inner dialogue. God knows our hearts and calls us, in love, toward healing and wholeness—toward His best for us—which includes not only our outward obedience but also our inner messaging. God's desire is that we would walk in freedom on the inside and outside. So, instead of offering help for personal discernment about specific issues, I want to focus our attention on some of the broader themes of God's will for all of us, which includes God's best for our thought lives.

> God knows our hearts and calls us, in love, toward healing and wholeness.

What does the term "God's will" mean to you?

Do you think it is possible for God to transform our thoughts? Why or why not?

Leaning into the Scripture

It is both exciting and humbling to me that God knows me so well, He knows my thoughts. Even more humbling is that He knows my thoughts and is still crazy about me. Am I alone in this? Am I the only one whose faith is bolstered because God sees us as whole and beautiful even though He knows our very broken and unbeautiful thoughts? I didn't think so!

There is no greater example of God knowing our thoughts than a story in Matthew 9 where Jesus is able to hear not only the thoughts and motives of those wanting to do good but also the thoughts and motives of those trying to do Him harm.

> *Jesus stepped into a boat, crossed over and came to his own town. ²Some men brought to him a paralyzed man, lying on a mat. When Jesus saw their faith, he said to the man, "Take heart, son; your sins are forgiven."*
>
> *³At this, some of the teachers of the law said to themselves, "This fellow is blaspheming!"*
>
> *⁴Knowing their thoughts, Jesus said, **"Why do you entertain evil thoughts in your hearts? ⁵Which is easier: to say, 'Your sins are forgiven,' or to say, 'Get up and walk'?** ⁶But I want you to know that the Son of Man has authority on earth to forgive sins." So he said to the paralyzed man, "Get up, take your mat and go home." ⁷Then the man got up and went home. ⁸When the crowd saw this, they were filled with awe; and they praised God, who had given such authority to man.*

(Matthew 9:1-8, emphasis added)

Jesus asks two questions to the teachers of the Law that speak to the heart of their spiritual problems (pun intended).

First, He asks:

"Why do you entertain evil thoughts in your hearts?" (v. 4).

I love that the translators of the New International Version used the verb "entertain" here. To entertain means "to hold in the mind," but the word also can mean "to have as a guest . . . show hospitality to."⁶

When we entertain evil thoughts and let them take root in us, we are allowing them to live rent-free in our minds and hearts. This is not just a problem for nonbelievers. Those of us who are in Christ yet continue to entertain negativity, gossip, fear, doubt, and shame in our brains are crowding out the truths of God in the process.

The apostle Paul's words in 2 Corinthians 10:5 offer this hope for our tendency to be "negativity entertainers": "We demolish arguments and every pretension that sets itself up against the knowledge of God, and we take captive every thought to make it obedient to Christ."

We do not have to entertain negativity but can take it captive. When harmful or destructive thoughts come into our heads (and they will)—when doubts creep in and fear grips us—we must "tie up" anything that is contrary to the truth of God so

it cannot run free in our cerebral cortex. In other words, with God's help we can root it out and then replace it with God's truth.

A friend of mine admitted that years ago he and his brothers tricked a babysitter to chase one of them outside while the other two locked the door behind her, pulled the running brother inside through a window, and closed the window before she could catch him, leaving her out in the cold until the parents got home.

While that is a terrible plan for babysitters, it is a brilliant strategy for combating those thoughts that discourage us. When negative inner messages erode our faith and try to control us, we can kick them out and lock the mental door behind them!

Jesus goes on to ask another question that emphasizes how much He prioritizes our motives over our motions:

"Which is easier: to say, 'Your sins are forgiven,' or to say, 'Get up and walk'?" (v. 5)

One is spiritual in nature, the other physical. Both are miraculous. Both allow us to walk in freedom. Yet these religious leaders were more concerned about Jesus's verbiage about the sins, totally forgetting to rejoice that the man who had been unable to walk when he awoke that morning now was able to walk and praise God with everyone else.

When and how have you been a "negativity entertainer"?

Practically speaking, how can you "take captive every thought" (2 Corinthians 10:5)?

Leaning into Hope

God's will and best for all of us is inner transformation. Obviously, inner transformation will lead to outer obedience, but often we get the order of operations confused. Sometimes we think that if we just *do* good, we will *be* good. If we just act kindly, then kindness will eventually follow. But God's will goes beyond the appearance of faith, calling each of us to inner peace and freedom. God is intimately acquainted with our inner thoughts yet offers us love, freedom, and grace, beckoning us toward heart change. This ongoing work of transformation (also called sanctification) is God's plan for each of us.

God accomplishes this transformation as He makes us into holy people. Though at times it may feel like a construction zone in our hearts, God's will for us is holiness and wholeness; and so God faithfully works in, around, and through us to accomplish this end. In Philippians 1:6, the apostle Paul offers this encouragement about this ongoing construction work of God: "He who began a good work in you will carry it on to completion until the day of Christ Jesus."

With this encouragement, we can rest in the knowledge that even though God knows our secret thoughts, He is not angry with us but calls us in love toward healing and wholeness in Christ.

Why do you think Jesus prioritizes the inner life over the outer one?

Has your heart been hardened in any way by hardships or challenges? If so, how?

How do you sense God inviting you to cooperate with His transforming inner work?

A Practical Next Step

Pray Psalm 139:23–24:

Search me, God, and know my heart; test me and know my anxious thoughts. / See if there is any offensive way in me, and lead me in the way everlasting.

What rises within you as you pray? Where are you in need of forgiveness and inner healing? How is God offering you grace and calling you toward heart change? What is a specific invitation of God for you in this moment?

Day 4 God's Plan for Us Is That We Serve Others

Jesus's Question:
"Which of these three do you think was a neighbor to the man who fell into the hands of robbers?"
(Luke 10:36)

The Question We Ask:
How can I be a good neighbor?

Leaning into the Question

The members of my family are huge *Star Wars* fans—like, Death Star huge. For those of you unfamiliar with the Lucas franchise and its characters, first, I offer my condolences. The movies, albeit imperfect, are a jaunt in imagination, a feast for the eyes, and a compelling narrative that spans generations. We have watched every cartoon spin-off, vintage television special, and interview with the actors we can find. We have spent countless hours reading books based on the *Star Wars* characters, playing board games with the *Star Wars* theme, and dressing at Halloween as some of the movie's most iconic characters.

When I was a kid, I wanted to be Princess Leia—with a giant twelve-pound braided bun above each ear and a sassy attitude. With my curly hair, I looked more like Chewbacca, but it did not stop me from reciting lines, practicing a British accent (kind of), and saving the galaxy, at least in my mind.

When one of the latest movies came out, we decided to wait until we could go as a family, but I was speaking out of town that weekend, so we had to wait almost a week before our schedules allowed our theatrical evening. We chose to abstain from television and social media to avoid any possible spoilers. The day we were to see the movie, our son came home deflated. When I probed for the possible reason behind his melancholy, he responded with "I can't believe Jimmy told me that Han Solo dies in this movie."

Han Solo had been a main staple in this movie franchise, and news of his death was devastating. *Devastating.*

Now there were two of us who felt deflated. We swore to keep our new knowledge to ourselves and not ruin it for the other two in the family, but I would be lying if I said that this new awareness did not, on some level, ruin the movie for me. There is something about knowing such an important plot that disallowed me to see the movie in the same way I would have without this knowledge; it forever changed how I viewed the story line.

Have you ever experienced something similar? How quickly a single comment can derail our personal plans and change our perspective forever. The same is true of a single question of Jesus.

Leaning into the Scripture

Even before I became a Christian, I was familiar with the story of the good Samaritan. It was often used, even in secular contexts, to describe a person who sacrificed money, time, and care for a person who is not their friend. But once I started to follow Jesus, I came to realize that this parable paints a story of so much more than just good deeds.

25On one occasion an expert in the law stood up to test Jesus. "Teacher," he asked, "what must I do to inherit eternal life?"

26"What is written in the Law?" he replied. "How do you read it?"

27He answered, "'Love the Lord your God with all your heart and with all your soul and with all your strength and with all your mind'; and, 'Love your neighbor as yourself.'"

28"You have answered correctly," Jesus replied. "Do this and you will live."

29But he wanted to justify himself, so he asked Jesus, "And who is my neighbor?"

30In reply Jesus said: "A man was going down from Jerusalem to Jericho, when he was attacked by robbers. They stripped him of his clothes, beat him and went away, leaving him half dead. 31A priest happened to be going down the same road, and when he saw the man, he passed by on the other side. 32So too, a Levite, when he came to the place and saw him, passed by on the other side. 33But a Samaritan, as he traveled, came where the man was; and when he saw him, he took pity on him. 34He went to him and bandaged his wounds, pouring on oil and wine. Then he put the man on his own donkey, brought him to an inn and took care of him. 35The next day he took out two denarii and gave them to the innkeeper. 'Look after him,' he said, 'and when I return, I will reimburse you for any extra expense you may have.'

³⁶**"Which of these three do you think was a neighbor to the man who fell into the hands of robbers?"**

³⁷*The expert in the law replied, "The one who had mercy on him."*

Jesus told him, "Go and do likewise."

(Luke 10:25-37, emphasis added)

> How does Jesus define being a good neighbor? *Sacrifice.*

Similar to the *Star Wars* truth grenade that my son threw on my lap, disallowing me to see the movie plot the same way, Jesus spoke such profound truth in the parable of the good Samaritan. Never again would his listeners be able to look at the definition of "neighbor" the same. Jesus asked, "Which of these three do you think was a neighbor to the man who fell into the hands of robbers?" (v. 36). He was drawing their attention not only to the fact that the man who helped was a Samaritan, an "enemy" of the Jews, but also that he was the one who was a good neighbor.

When we refuse to allow someone to break into traffic, feel justified in our anger when someone receives accolades we think we deserve, are perturbed when a new line opens up in the grocery store and people behind us run to the new, shorter line (I hate this one!), or feel pride when we win, we are not practicing good neighbor-ing. (Now, I know that is not really a word, but you get the idea.)

How does Jesus define being a good neighbor? *Sacrifice.* His question cuts right to the quick. In other words, *Are you willing to put your needs, time, plans, and resources on the back burner so that another person—even an enemy—might see the love of God through your actions?*

My son may have ruined a movie, but Jesus's question in Luke 10 forever ruined the world's definition of neighbor—in a good way.

What do you know about the historical background of the relationship between the Jews and the Samaritans? Why was this context important to understand in this parable?

What common-day examples can you give for similar rivalries and animosity?

Leaning into Hope

It is easy in today's culture to get a case of the UNs—feelings of inadequacy that include *un*acceptable, *un*helpful, *un*derperforming, *un*-special, *un*derprepared, *un*safe, *un*fun, *un*productive, *un*approved, *un*comfortable, and *un*faithful.

These UNs are not of the Lord. In fact, the way He lived His life on earth flew in the face of this list.

Jesus's question in Luke 10 clarifies that serving our neighbor is not as much about what we do as who we accommodate. It is not about the UNs of productivity but about how God produces fruit in us. It is not about any accolades we receive but about the assistance we offer those in need. It is not about the UNs of importance in the eyes of the world but the important work we can do in Jesus's name when we follow Him. We can find hope in knowing that each day provides opportunities for this kind of sacrificial service—and sufficient grace when we make mistakes.

In order to practice "neighboring" from a place of love and leave the UNs of the world behind, we must receive God's love and see ourselves as "the beloved" so that we may serve from a healthy perspective. When we know that God loves us and live from this place, we can serve others in love.

What words or ideas come to mind when you think of a being a neighbor who serves others sacrificially? Are they positive or negative? List them below:

Positive   *Negative*

In your opinion, what does serving and loving one's neighbor look like, practically speaking? How might you show neighboring in your everyday life?

How did Jesus show neighboring in His life?

Jesus set an example of being a good neighbor to you when He died on the cross—the greatest act of sacrificial love. Do you ever struggle to receive God's love and see yourself as "the beloved"? If so, what do you think is keeping you from letting God love you?

A Practical Next Step

Being a neighbor following the example of Christ is not self-deprecation but humble servanthood made possible because of our confidence in our identity in Him and His unconditional love for us. To neighbor others well in love, we must see ourselves as the beloved.

Prayerfully make three lists:

1. The lies you "entertain" frequently.
2. What helps you to see yourself as the beloved—to receive the love of God.
3. Three ways you can practice being a good neighbor this week.

Ask God to help you serve and love others from your identity as His beloved.

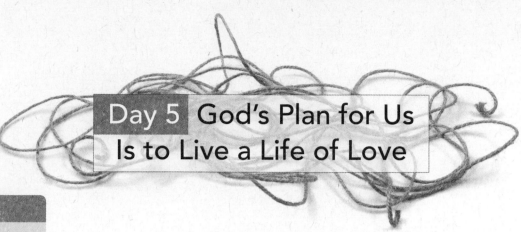

Day 5 God's Plan for Us Is to Live a Life of Love

Jesus's Question:
"Simon son of John, do you love me more than these? . . .
Simon son of John, do you love me? . . .
Simon son of John, do you love me?"
(John 21:15-17)

The Question We Ask:
What does loving Jesus look like?

Leaning into the Question

We are a competitive family. Not the type who has a thousand athletic awards and trophies on the mantle. Not the kind that hosts board game tournaments for humble friends and family alike.

We are competitive with expressing love. The "script" reads something like this:

"I love you."
"I love you more."
"I love you most."
"I love you mostest."
"I love you mostester."
"I love you mostestest."

It gets ridiculous.

I often end the battle with "I love you around Jesus and back" (because that is infinite).

Now, we are clear that such exchanges are fraught with bad grammar and ridiculousness, but we love this competitive engagement.

What we do not always love is to follow Romans 12:10 (NRSVUE): "Love one another with mutual affection; *outdo one another in showing honor.*"

We love to say it regularly, but we do not always show it regularly.

It could be as simple as taking out the trash without being asked. Or not putting a dirty dish in the sink when the dishwasher was just loaded (OK, that one makes me crazy). Or making sure the toilet seat is wiped down for the next person.

Or not getting bitter and resentful when the above occurs or does not occur (this one is 100,000 percent me; I am guilty of this the mostesterest).

I am glad that God does not get bitter and resentful against those who claim to love Him when we do not do what He has called us to do. God's grace is one of the many ways He proves that He loves us the "mostesterest."

In today's story, we are going to examine Peter, one of Jesus's friends and disciples who loved with his heart and mouth, but who had trouble putting his words into practice when the going got rough.

Leaning into the Scripture

After Jesus's death, burial, and resurrection, the risen Jesus has an exchange with Peter, the disciple who loved Jesus fiercely, defended Him adamantly, and then denied Him quickly after Jesus's arrest. In this encounter, Jesus joins a group of the disciples in the early morning after a night of fishing. He prepares breakfast on the shore for them—fish and bread—and then after breakfast He talks with Peter.

*15"When they had finished eating, Jesus said to Simon Peter, **"Simon son of John, do you love me more than these?"***

"Yes, Lord," he said, "you know that I love you."

Jesus said, "Feed my lambs."

*16Again Jesus said, **"Simon son of John, do you love me?"***

He answered, "Yes, Lord, you know that I love you."

Jesus said, "Take care of my sheep."

*17The third time he said to him, **"Simon son of John, do you love me?"***

Peter was hurt because Jesus asked him the third time, "Do you love me?" He said, "Lord, you know all things; you know that I love you."

Jesus said, "Feed my sheep. 18Very truly I tell you, when you were younger you dressed yourself and went where you wanted; but when you are old you will stretch out your hands, and someone else will dress you and lead you where you do not want to go." 19Jesus said this to indicate the kind of death by which Peter would glorify God. Then he said to him, "Follow me!"

(John 21:15-19, emphasis added)

At the beginning of this exchange, it sounds a little like one of our family love battles. Repeated questions. Repeated answers. But if we look closely, we see that Jesus asks Peter about his devotion three times—a significant number for Peter because that is the number of times Peter denied Jesus, just as Jesus had prophesied he would.

We also see here that Jesus is making a correlation between feeling and action, between loving Him and feeding His sheep. Peter does love Jesus, but Jesus calls him to something "mostester"—service overflowing from love.

Jesus's repeated questions must have broken Peter's heart. Perhaps it seemed to Peter that Jesus did not believe his answers the first or second time. Surely Jesus's questions brought up Peter's denials and shame. Yet Jesus's questions were intentional, both offering Peter forgiveness and stoking the fire within for service— concurrently.

We are not unlike Peter, you and me.

- Sometimes in our actions or decisions, we deny Him. Yet because of His great love for us, Jesus gives us grace by acknowledging us.
- Sometimes we get ahead of ourselves, overpromising and underdelivering with the Lord. Yet because of His great love for us, Jesus gives us grace by offering us patience.
- Sometimes we lie. Yet because of His great love for us, Jesus gives us grace by reminding us of truth.

Just as He called Peter to an even higher calling—to feed His sheep—so He calls you and me to deeper faith, greater obedience, and richer love each and every day.

Leaning into Hope

Jesus's series of questions to Peter point us to a practical way we can show Him not only how much we love Him but also how much we can love others in response to His love: *Feed my sheep.*

While many of the verses we have explored in our study have focused on the interior spiritual life, here we find Jesus naming a way our inner spiritual life becomes practical—"feeding sheep." Who are Jesus's sheep? Those who hear His voice and follow Him. *How are we to feed them?* With actual food, encouragement, time, sacrifice, kindness, and a million other ways.

Though there are endless ways to feed the sheep of God, here are a few ideas using the acronym SHEEP:

Share	generously with others
Hear	what others have to say
Encourage	others
Entreat	God on behalf of others
Practice	kindness to others

To put it simply, feeding Jesus's sheep is living a life of love following His example. It is . . .

- praying as Jesus prayed,
- healing as Jesus healed,
- comforting as Jesus comforted,
- encouraging as Jesus encouraged,
- teaching as Jesus taught,
- empowering as Jesus empowered, and
- trusting God as Jesus trusted.

When we choose to follow Jesus, we are choosing a life of love and service. And this is possible only because we love Jesus. Loving Jesus means loving others.

> When we choose to follow Jesus, we are choosing a life of love and service.

How would you explain what it means to live a life of love?

What are some ways we can feed Jesus's sheep? Add to the list of ideas in today's lesson.

How would an observer of your life know that you follow and love Jesus?

Where is God leading you to feed His sheep in this season?

A Practical Next Step

Romans 12:10 in The Message (MSG) translation says this:

> *Love from the center of who you are; don't fake it. Run for dear life from evil; hold on for dear life to good. Be good friends who love deeply; practice playing second fiddle.*

Write this verse (in the version you most appreciate) on three sticky notes and place them in locations where you will see them often. Memorize the verse and make it a personal prayer.

Week 5 | Wrap-up

The university I attended partnered with the local church and started a group just for students. It was called Campus After Dark, and the weekly worship service included music from the music pastor at one of the largest churches in North America (he flew in to Phoenix each week) and a preacher from one of the huge local churches. It was amazing. I had never attended services just for youth or young adults, and the experience was life giving for me. It was thrilling to participate in a service where people in my season of life were worshiping and learning together. I am open to learning from people in all stages of life, but the messages and music were tailored to minister especially to my generation.

The preacher was so charismatic—not a denominational descriptor but a general adjective. He was an insightful, engaging, and wise storyteller who would command our attention by investing in us and staying faithful to the Word. He loved the Bible, and every session displayed that more and more.

I was eager to hear his sermon on the topic of heaven. As a person who did not grow up in a family that talked about an afterlife, heaven was mystical, mysterious, and muddy in my thinking. People in white robes strumming harps all day did not seem enticing, and yet this was the depiction of heaven I had been given.

But when this preacher told a story about heaven, it gave my brain something I could hold on to regarding the Pearly Gates.

He told the fascinated crowd about his childhood, his siblings, and some of his family traditions, including a yearly visit to his grandmother's house each Thanksgiving. He talked about the food he would enjoy there, and he said that after dessert, his grandmother would ask him and his brothers to check under the old house in which she lived. She was too old and feeble to wriggle freely in the limited crawl space under the house, but she gave them various responsibilities to check on plumbing and the like while under the huge house. He talked about how cool it was to army-crawl under the house and see all the spiderwebs and the massive labyrinth of plumbing and wiring.

After they had investigated the things that needed checking, he would sit with his brothers on the porch with Grandma and talk about heaven. First, she would ask the boys if they enjoyed dinner and their time together. Then she would thank them for the work they had done under the house. She would ask them to describe what it was like under the house, listening intently to each adjective and detail. They knew what was coming next. It was as much of a tradition as the turkey, stuffing, and mashed potatoes on the Thanksgiving dinner table.

She would tell them that her house was a little like heaven. The fellowship and celebrations will be amazing, but right now, here on earth, we only get glimpses of the underside of eternity. We are only in the crawl space of eternity, but someday, we will no longer be trapped, wriggling and limited to the confines of the space called earth. Instead, we will sit at the Banquet Table of Eternity with God. We have a job to do while we are here, but someday we will be free to enjoy all that God has prepared for us in heaven.

He may have been making that story up, but I bought it.

And when I feel frustrated by the limitations of my body or the spiderwebs of life, I remind myself that I am in the underbelly of heaven now, but someday I will have the freedom and bliss of being in the presence of my Lord and Savior.

This week, we have focused on some general components of God's plan for our lives. Ultimately, He wants us to spend eternity with Him in heaven. But eternal life actually begins *now*. In this life, God plans for us to have enduring faith, to know we have hope and a future, to experience inner transformation, to serve others, and to live a life of love. I'm in! How about you?

> God plans for us to have enduring faith, to know we have hope and a future, to experience inner transformation, to serve others, and to live a life of love.

Of the questions we've explored, which one resonates most, and why?

What questions do you still have related to following Christ?

Read the week's memory verse, Psalm 25:4-5, slowly several times. Is there a word or phrase that catches your attention or touches your heart? What does God have to say to you about the word or phrase in light of your current life experience? How is God inviting you to respond?

Video Viewer Guide Week 5

What Is God's Plan for Us?

Memory Verse:

Psalm 25:4-5 NIV

Open eyes:

_____ me your ways, LORD,

teach me your paths.

Open mind:

_____ me in your truth and _____ me.

Open heart:

…for you are God my Savior,

and my _____ is in you all day long.

Permission Slip:

This week, we have focused on some non-specific components of God's plan for our lives—some irrefutable truths about what God wants for all of His people. Ultimately, He wants us to spend eternity with Him in heaven. But eternal life actually begins now. God plans for us to have enduring faith, to know we have hope and a future, to experience inner transformation, to serve others, and to live a life of love that begins today if our hearts are open to Him as our guide and Savior.

You have permission to feel _____

What Does It Mean to Follow God?

MEMORY VERSE:

He has shown you, O mortal, what is good. And what does the Lord require of you? / To act justly and to love mercy and to walk humbly with your God.

(Micah 6:8)

This is going to make me sound old, but there was a time that buying a shirt was more expensive than having it dry cleaned. I am a bargain shopper, but there is nothing that hurts my heart (and my wallet) more than to spend $83 at the dry cleaner's to get my $26 blouse dry-cleaned.

When Scott and I were first wed, he often took his Sunday clothes to the dry cleaner. His responsibilities as a worship pastor at the time included rocking a suit, so that meant that, periodically, those threads needed some TLC.

There was a family-owned dry cleaner down the street from our church. The family always greeted me with a smile, remembering my name as I dropped off Scott's shirts. Before taking the clothes to the back, they would promptly staple a number to the tag of each garment, making sure it would return to the proper owner.

At first, I thought the number identified their business. But after inquiring, I found out that every family on their roster of patrons was assigned a number. They knew to whom each garment belonged because it was marked accordingly.

Not unlike those shirts from long ago, you and I are marked by the blood of Jesus. As those set apart because of His grace, we belong to Him and are in Him; and others should be able to discern our identity by our actions, good deeds, kindness, and love. The way we live indicates that we are followers of God.

If you have questions about what it means to follow God—and your ability to do so—you are not alone! Even folks in the Bible had such questions and struggles. David was strong, handsome, capable, and musical. He was a shepherd, court minstrel, soldier, leader, and king. He also did his fair share of struggling to do what God required of him.

In the many psalms he wrote, David shares a myriad of questions about responsibility, faith, and pain, including feelings of betrayal. He is honest about his questions, pouring out his heart to the Lord in his anguish. David understands what it means to follow God yet is candid about the struggles such obedience can bring. Known as a man after God's own heart (see 1 Samuel 13:14 and Acts 13:22), David is unafraid to dig deeply, emote, communicate, inquire, and celebrate with God. He is a poet, a worshiper, an honest sojourner of faith, and a man marked by the love of God.

Like David, we are called to be women after God's own heart—women who are marked by the love of God and known to be God's followers by the way we live our lives. This week we will consider just a few examples of what this means: offering compassion instead of judgment, being humble, practicing empathy, being born of the Spirit, and taking up our cross. In these ways we can fulfill the call of Micah 6:8—to act justly, love mercy, and walk humbly with our God.

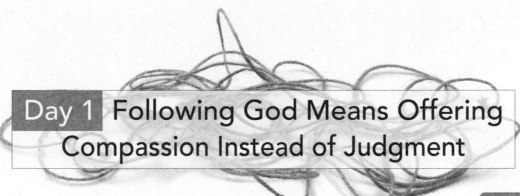

Day 1 Following God Means Offering Compassion Instead of Judgment

Big Idea

God calls us to love others in the same way that He loves us.

Jesus's Question:

"Why do you see the splinter that's in your brother's or sister's eye, but don't notice the log in your own eye? How can you say to your brother or sister, 'Let me take the splinter out of your eye,' when there's a log in your own eye?"
(Matthew 7:3-4 CEB)

The Question We Ask:

What does Jesus say about judging others?

Leaning into the Question

I love to hike. There is something about getting outside, enjoying nature, and getting blood pumping that makes my heart sing. I am not the type of hiker who carries a giant pack or traverses mountainsides—that's rock climbing, and I have zero interest in that; that is for people who are actually in shape, not just have a shape.

In Arizona, hikers often come across snakes. In fact, there are dog trainers who actually train dogs to avoid rattlers, since unsuspecting dogs accompanying their owners on hikes are often the victims of snakebites.

Although my heart rate takes half an hour to return to its regular rhythm after seeing one of these slithery creatures, I haven't yet had what I would call a super scary encounter with a snake. I did come across an eight-foot albino snake at a camp at which I served. It was beautiful and was clearly someone's pet who had made a prison break. It showed zero interest in me, even after I took out my camera and snapped a ridiculous number of pictures.

My biggest issue is my complete ignorance about the types of snakes we have in my state. They all look scary to me. I know that I should pay more attention, but on a hike I am often just trying to breathe without passing out.

The Arizona coral snake is known for its distinct coloring—a pattern of black, yellow, and red rings encircling the entirety of the snake's body, differentiating this venomous snake from nonvenomous snakes. It is usually less than two feet in length and has a shy demeanor. I have only seen one in the zoo, but when I came across one of its nonvenomous doppelgangers on a

hike one time, I panicked (and by panicked, I mean I may have struggled with both volume and bladder control!).

I tried to recall the nursery rhyme my fifth-grade teacher taught us students to help us remember the coloring of this snake as an indicator of its danger, but I was so flustered in the moment that I began making erroneous rhymes to try to calm myself down. Unfortunately, that didn't help. When I got home, I looked up the rhyme and committed it to memory. My future hiker-self will thank me for it.

"Red on black, friend of Jack. Red on yellow, unlucky fellow."

If only dangerous people were as easy to distinguish. Instead, we are complicated creatures. Shaped by our personalities, experiences, traumas, and choices, we are a menagerie of past, present, and potential. Even those of us who are in Christ and have been redeemed are still in process; we have not completely shed the habits, hang-ups, and hurts from our past, which means we do not always play well with others.

And when we are struggling, we are more likely to judge others. In our insecurity, we may lash out at another to try and take the attention off our own inadequacies. Or in my case, the things I like least about myself are the first places I jump to judge others.

> **When unchecked by love and grace, our confidence in being called and adored by God can turn into an attitude of superiority.**

God, who is a righteous judge (Psalm 7:11) has every right to judge the wicked because He is blameless. Yet He "demonstrates his own love for us in this: While we were still sinners, Christ died for us" (Romans 5:8). He leads with love. As His followers, we should do likewise.

Leaning into the Scripture

In the Sermon on the Mount, Jesus addresses our tendency to judge others.

> *"Do not judge, or you too will be judged. For in the same way you judge others, you will be judged, and with the measure you use, it will be measured to you.*
>
> *"Why do you look at the speck of sawdust in your brother's eye and pay no attention to the plank in your own eye? How can you say to your brother, 'Let me take the speck out of your eye,' when all the time there is a plank in your own eye? You hypocrite, first take the plank out of your own eye, and then you will see clearly to remove the speck from your brother's eye."*
>
> (Matthew 7:1-5 CEB)

When I am being judgmental of others, hearing this series of questions pierces my heart. The truth is, when I find myself being Judgy McJudgerton toward another, it is usually because they are doing something that I wish I could do and am envious of, I have done before and am feeling shame about, or I realize is evidence I'm "running on religion" instead of embracing and extending the love and grace of God.

Can you relate?

I love the visual that Jesus uses here: a speck of sawdust versus a two-by-four. The visual is almost comical: a plank coming out of a person's eye would be comedy gold—if it wasn't so serious, that is.

But I think the question gets more pointed when it involves the *how*—how we handle the speck in the eye of a fellow believer with judgment and shortsightedness (see what I did there?).

A former pastor of mine shed new light on this concept for me. He said that when we are removing something from the eye of another, often we are gentle, get very close, lower our voices, become very reassuring, and are careful in our procedures.

Jesus's point is that such care is how our posture should be when we are acting in love. This is not how we are when being judgmental, but it's how we should be when addressing the sin in others' lives. The honest truth is that if I am actually removing a splinter from someone's eye, I may practice such gentle care, but when I am in a posture of judgment toward another, I am nary of those things! I am not gentle or close or soft-spoken or reassuring or careful. Rather, when I am being judgmental, I'm often criticizing from a distance with prideful flair, making my opinion known, and showing no concern for the other person.

Recently I saw a comic that made me both smile and cry a little. It shows the apostle Peter in front of the gates to heaven. There is a man waiting to get in, but the apostle says to him, "You were a believer, yes, but you skipped the not-being-a-jerk-about-it part."

When I pulled this comic up on my computer, the following related searches popped up:

Why Are Christians So Mean?
5 Signs of Spiritual Maturity . . . That Actually Show You Lack It
If God Is Love, Don't Be a Jerk

Although this comic was penned in 2007, it still seems to be relevant, doesn't it?

When unchecked by love and grace, our confidence in being called and adored by God can turn into an attitude of superiority. When unchecked by love and grace, the affirmation of our value as one redeemed by the Lord can lead to devaluing others. So, how do we keep ourselves in check?

Let's start by drilling down into the verse for insight into three *R*s that can help us to steer clear of judgment and embrace compassion instead.

1. Relationship

"Why do you look at the speck of sawdust in your brother's eye and pay no attention to the plank in your own eye?"

(Matthew 7:3a)

With this question, Jesus points out that focusing on the imperfections, limitations, or sins of a brother or sister in Christ leads to judgment, which is corrosive to a relationship.

If we are going to love others well and avoid judging others unfairly, we need to keep our eyes focused on the mercy God has for them rather than on the sawdust of their sin.

Notice that Jesus did not say that it was OK for the sawdust in the eye of our brother to stay there. When people go against God's best for them and disobey His Word, it is not that we are to ignore it; that can do more damage to both their eye and their relationship with God. We are called to *lovingly* "spur one another on toward love and good deeds" (Hebrews 10:24).

In my life, this often takes shape most clearly when I am on social media. The beauty of platforms such as Facebook and Instagram is that I can stay in touch my followers, friends, and family. But the downside is that I also get to stay in touch with some of their poor choices. I have found that making a blanket post or slapping on a Bible verse has not changed a single mind; however, reaching out humbly, prayerfully asking them to meet for coffee, and truly caring about them before talking about their choices is a much more loving way to help them become aware of the sawdust situation.

2. Reality

The second part of Jesus's question gets to the reality that should be the focus of our attention instead:

> *"How can you say to your brother or sister, 'Let me take the splinter out of your eye,' when there's a log in your own eye?"*

> (Matthew 7:4 CEB)

The contrast of log and splinter reminds us that both splinters and logs are an issue, and either way, loving others does not include disregarding our own issues for the sake of pointing out the issues of another. It reminds us that the primary issue is our own sin. Jesus wants us to focus on our own issues, rather than pointing out those of others. The reality is that the only person we can change is ourselves. Often focusing on others' sin is a way to avoid or deny our own. If we are going to love others well, we need to keep our eyes on the reservoir of mercy God has for us and serve others from that reservoir.

In my own life, this sometimes takes the form of writing out a fearless moral inventory. It is a practice I was taught years ago in a church-wide campaign, and it involves journaling all the sins I commit in a day. The fact that I cannot contain all my daily sins on one side of a piece of paper is a good indicator that I still have some growing to do. But the realization and contemplation of my imperfection make me much less willing to jump in and judge the wrongdoings of another without humility.

3. Restraint

"You hypocrite, first take the plank out of your own eye, and then you will see clearly to remove the speck from your brother's eye."

(Matthew 7:5)

Jesus calls each of us to exercise caution and restraint when seeing errors in others. He knows that such hypocrisy is divisive to the church and to our relationships.

Only once we have acknowledged and addressed our own sin are we in a humble posture to point out the sin of others. Even then we should do so gently and with caution. As my former pastor instructed, do this gently, closely, with lowered and reassuring voices, and carefully.

In my life, this means committing myself to invest in a person before I make the withdrawal of judgment. Spending time together, doing acts of kindness, having good conversations, attempting to understand them better, truly listening, and praying for wisdom need to occur before I share careful guidance. Only after these actions do I feel that I have the right to speak into the life of another and call them to God's best for them.

These three filters—relationship, reality, and restraint—do not give us permission to live recklessly, disobey God's Word, or let brothers and sisters in Christ do likewise. Rather, they remind us that Jesus provides parameters to help us avoid judgment and handle imperfections in our own lives and the lives of others in a healthy and effective way.

From your perspective, how does it feel to be judged? Recall a time when you were judged and describe how you felt.

Recall a time when you judged another. How did you feel initially? How did you feel later?

When or for what reasons do you find yourself judging others?

How has judging others affected your relationships?

Leaning into Hope

Matthew 7:1-2 instructs us, "Do not judge, or you too will be judged. For in the same way you judge others, you will be judged, and with the measure you use, it will be measured to you." God calls us to love others as He loves us—with compassion and grace. This verse is not saying God will judge us as we judge others—because God is not like us. God is love. Romans 5:8 tells us, "While we were still sinners, Christ died for us." Jesus's words here in Matthew 7 suggest that others will treat us as we have treated them. This is relationship 101. He is teaching us how to love others.

You and I have hope because of the example of God. He is perfect, blameless, loving, and true—things we are not.

The apostle Paul said it this way:

> You, therefore, have no excuse, you who pass judgment on someone else, for at whatever point you judge another, you are condemning yourself, because you who pass judgment do the same things. ²Now we know that God's judgment against those who do such things is based on truth. ³So when you, a mere human being, pass judgment on them and yet do the same things, do you think you will escape God's judgment? ⁴Or do you show contempt for the riches of his kindness, forbearance and patience, not realizing that God's kindness is intended to lead you to repentance?
>
> (Romans 2:1-4)

It is God's kindness that leads to our repentance. God has every right to judge as the only perfect One, yet His tool of choice to lead us to Himself is kindness. Not a snarky social media post. Not a billboard condemning the actions of others. Not hate speech. But kindness.

And He calls us to love others in the same way that He loves us.

Have you ever had someone love you enough to humbly point out a poor choice or sin pattern? If so, how did they do it, and how did you respond?

Have you ever come alongside another and lovingly pointed them to truth? Did your attempts move them to repentance? Why or why not?

Which of the three *R*s resonates most closely with your tendency?

A Practical Next Step

Is there someone you have been judging (whether or not they know it)? Often the faults we most easily identify in others are things we struggle with ourselves—whether or not we are aware of it. What is it about this person that irritates or offends you? Talk with God about it, asking Him to reveal how this "speck of sawdust" in someone else's eye might reveal a "plank" in your own. How is God inviting you to address your own issue? How is God calling you to offer compassion to the person you named? You might consider journaling your conversation with God for deeper exploration.

Day 2 Following God Means Practicing Empathy

Big Idea

Empathizing with others helps us to love them.

Jesus's Question:
"Do you see this woman?"
(Luke 7:44)

The Question We Ask:
How can I see others as Jesus sees them?

Leaning into the Question

I love reading old stories. Stories of outlaws from the Wild West. Stories of theatrical escapades in Shakespearean time. Stories of courage and determination from the American settlers. But I also love a juicy, quirky story about interpersonal relationships gone wrong. One such story comes from San Francisco—and as a girl who spent her elementary school years in Northern California, this story grabbed my attention.

German immigrant Nicholas Yung moved to the United States in 1848, started a mortuary business in California, and bought a beautiful yet modest home there with his wife, Rosina. Together they enjoyed the California sunshine, a beautiful garden, the fruit of their labor, and a pretty fantastic existence—that is, until Charles Crocker, a rich and petty man, moved in next door.

Crocker was one of four men who established the Central Railroad, a lucrative investment that gave Crocker the financial wherewithal to gobble up properties, which he did. He and his business partners began purchasing the residences on what was then called California Street Hill, renaming it Nob Hill. Crocker erected a 12,000-square-foot mansion, but the one thing he could not seem to build was a good relationship with his new neighbor, Nicholas Yung, who refused to sell his space on the northeast corner of the block. Although there are various accounts of their disputes over the land, the bottom line is that Yung would not give up his beloved home and Crocker would not relent in his pursuit.

Used to getting what he wanted, Crocker was infuriated by the neighbor who refused to acquiesce. He ordered his workers, as they razed the block, to position their dynamite blasts so that the debris of rock would bombard the home of Yung. This fueled Yung's resolve even more. He

became obnoxious in his negotiating methods with Crocker, but the tycoon had the resources to make life difficult for Yung—which he did.

Crocker had his workforce erect a wooden fence with forty-foot panels on his land, towering over three sides of Yung's property. The behemoth fence blotted out the sun and cool air to Yung's home, leaving the couple in darkness. Their once beautiful garden wilted. The *San Francisco Chronicle* called the massive fencing a "memorial of malignity and malevolence."[1] The feud between the two neighbors drew so much attention that tourists would take the cable car and ride up to Nob Hill just to gawk at the monstrous fence.

Yung and his family finally moved out but still would not sell the property to Crocker. After Yung's passing in 1880, his widow refused to cave in, even after their once idyllic home became a vacant lot and a magnet for litter. Only after her death was the property finally sold to the Crocker family.

In a twist of fate, an earthquake and subsequent fire in 1906 destroyed much of Nob Hill, gutting the Crocker mansion and its neighboring buildings. Rather than rebuild the giant structures, the descendants of the power-hungry Crocker donated the block to charity. The very location for years of feuding and spite became an epicenter of hope: a church.[2]

Crocker refused to see the value and plight of his neighbor. He lacked empathy, the ability to understand, connect to, and share the feelings of another. We see a similar stance in the Pharisee who invited Jesus to a dinner at his house.

Leaning into the Scripture

As we've seen, the Pharisees were a group of religious leaders in power at the time of Jesus. We are not sure why this man, Simon, invited Jesus to his home, but we can be certain that a man who makes his living upholding the laws and traditions of the day did not expect to learn from the example of a sinful woman.

> [36]When one of the Pharisees invited Jesus to have dinner with him, he went to the Pharisee's house and reclined at the table. [37]A woman in that town who lived a sinful life learned that Jesus was eating at the Pharisee's house, so she came there with an alabaster jar of perfume. [38]As she stood behind him at his feet weeping, she began to wet his feet with her tears. Then she wiped them with her hair, kissed them and poured perfume on them.

> [39]When the Pharisee who had invited him saw this, he said to himself, "If this man were a prophet, he would know who is touching him and what kind of woman she is—that she is a sinner."

> [40]Jesus answered him, "Simon, I have something to tell you."

"Tell me, teacher," he said.

⁴¹"Two people owed money to a certain moneylender. One owed him five hundred denarii, and the other fifty. ⁴²Neither of them had the money to pay him back, so he forgave the debts of both. Now which of them will love him more?"

⁴³Simon replied, "I suppose the one who had the bigger debt forgiven."

"You have judged correctly," Jesus said.

⁴⁴Then he turned toward the woman and said to Simon, **"Do you see this woman?** I came into your house. You did not give me any water for my feet, but she wet my feet with her tears and wiped them with her hair. ⁴⁵You did not give me a kiss, but this woman, from the time I entered, has not stopped kissing my feet. ⁴⁶You did not put oil on my head, but she has poured perfume on my feet. ⁴⁷Therefore, I tell you, her many sins have been forgiven—as her great love has shown. But whoever has been forgiven little loves little."

(Luke 7:36-47, emphasis added)

> God calls us to empathize rather than judge because empathy helps us to love others as we are loved.

Simon the Pharisee failed to recognize this woman's value and worth and identify with her situation and feelings. He lacked empathy—perhaps because he was unaware of his own sin and great need for forgiveness. In any case, he failed to see her.

Jesus's question reveals that He not only saw this woman and was empathetic to her plight but also called others to do the same.

Have you ever felt unseen? Undervalued?

When was the last time you could totally relate to something someone shared (a loss, the anxiety of a new job, a frustration, etc.)? Did you feel more connected to that person? Why or why not?

How does it make you feel to realize that Jesus saw this woman, despite her past failures?

Leaning into Hope

We all have felt unseen. We all have felt disregarded, unimportant, insufficient, sidelined, and underappreciated at one time or another. The extravagant act of worship of this sinful woman is evidence that she was keenly aware of her bad choices and the goodness of Jesus, but Simon the Pharisee focused only on her sin, pointing it out and shaming her. He failed to see the woman behind the woe, the individual behind the iniquity, the miss behind the misdeed.

But it is the woman in this story I appreciate most, because her story is my story. Before I met Jesus, I made some terrible, horrible, no good, very bad decisions (props to Judith Viorst and her wonderful book *Alexander and the Terrible, Horrible, No Good, Very Bad Day*). Heck, I still do sometimes. It is easy for me to think that God loves me less as a result and takes His eyes off me in disappointment. Yet this story draws me back to the truth. It points out that Jesus knew this woman and her rotten past and chose to truly see her anyway. That's what Jesus does. That is what love does.

Jesus's love must have filled her with equal parts thankfulness (for the forgiveness) and humility (a realistic desire to do better) because that is how I feel when I receive God's forgiveness for my transgressions. And here is the beautiful part. As I receive the love and forgiveness of God, I'm able to offer that same love and forgiveness to others.

God calls us to empathize rather than judge because empathy helps us to love others as we are loved.

When have you most related to the woman in this story?

When have you most related to the Pharisee?

When have you most related to Jesus as he advocated for another?

A Practical Next Step

This woman was willing to sacrifice her reputation, her valuables, her pride, and her comfort to worship Jesus. He was willing to sacrifice His life for her to walk in freedom and empathize with others.

For what has God forgiven you that can help you to empathize with and love others, drawing them to Him? Make a list below. Then give thanks once again, basking in God's amazing love and grace!

Day 3 Following God Means Being Humble

Jesus's Question:
"What were you arguing about on the road?"
(Mark 9:33)

The Question We Ask:
What does humility look like?

Leaning into the Question

I love Christmas! I love all the food, decorations, carols, pageants, cookies, school programs, television specials, and traditions. Jesus picked a very busy time of year to have a birthday, right? All joking aside, and despite its busyness, the month before Christmas is by far my favorite time of the year.

My family own over one hundred nativities from all over the world, in differing shapes and sizes. We have two Christmas trees, stocking collections, and tree decorations for five different themes. But one of my favorite decorations is an Advent tree. It is positioned in the middle of our dining room table, and each day we locate the proper number and place the corresponding star, present, angel, or ornament on the tree.

Are there prettier decorations? Yes.

Are there decorations that have a higher monetary value? Yes.

Could I love this Advent tree more? Not sure.

Why do I love it so? It is a daily reminder to find value in each day and make every day truly count. Putting ornaments on this metal tree each day encourages the members of my family to see the special and unique components of each day and to tap into our thankfulness, but also to not forget to focus on the center of each of the nativities—Jesus—and the humility to which He calls us.

Humility is a vital component of being a follower of God, and thanking God for the potential to serve others each day is a good step toward greatness.

Jesus did not come to be depicted in a million nativities in my home, but instead, to set an example as a servant, a humble servant in the manger, on the road, on the cross, out of the tomb, and in our lives.

Paul wrote to the church in Philippi about this incredible servitude in Philippians 2:

Therefore if you have any encouragement from being united with Christ, if any comfort from his love, if any common sharing in the Spirit, if any tenderness and compassion, ²then make my joy complete by being like-minded, having the same love, being one in spirit and of one mind. ³Do nothing out of selfish ambition or vain conceit. Rather, in humility value others above yourselves, ⁴not looking to your own interests but each of you to the interests of the others.

⁵In your relationships with one another, have the same mindset as Christ Jesus:

⁶Who, being in very nature God,
    did not consider equality with God something to be used to his own
    advantage;
⁷rather, he made himself nothing
    by taking the very nature of a servant,
    being made in human likeness.
⁸And being found in appearance as a man,
    he humbled himself
    by becoming obedient to death—
        even death on a cross!

⁹Therefore God exalted him to the highest place
    and gave him the name that is above every name,
¹⁰that at the name of Jesus every knee should bow,
    in heaven and on earth and under the earth,
¹¹and every tongue acknowledge that Jesus Christ is Lord,
    to the glory of God the Father.

(Philippians 2:1-11)

Wow. The maker of heaven and earth. The One who made the stars in the sky, the beauty of flowers, the creatures of the ocean, and the person who invented Häagen-Dazs ice cream humbled Himself and made Himself a servant. The One who made the highest peak on Mount Everest became the lowest. The One who made the greatest impact on all humanity became the least of them. And He asks us to do likewise. Yet sometimes we have a hard time doing just that.

194

I spent way too much time trying to act cool in junior high and high school. I was 5'11" in fifth grade. I always carried extra weight, did not wear the coolest clothes, and was always too loud to be in the popular crowd.

But I wanted to be cool *so much*. One year, during the time of homecoming royalty campaigns, I tried to scheme some of the girls on my cheerleading squad for their votes, promising to vote for them for homecoming queen. Problem is, I had only one vote, and I am a terrible liar. They all found out, and I actually lost the few cool points I had in an attempt to look popular. Busted.

I am not the only one who struggled to follow the example of Jesus as a servant. As we saw in Week 5, Day 4, even His apostles, the twelve who spent the most time with Him, struggled to follow His call to be servants. Last week we explored the story in Mark's Gospel with a theme of serving others, and this week we're going to examine it in Luke's Gospel with the theme of humility, because this is perhaps one of the most persistent struggles we face in our performance-driven culture today. Like the disciples, we struggle not with how to be less but how to be best. In every area of life we are encouraged to strive to be the best, and social media only compounds the struggle.

Leaning into the Scripture

It seems that some of the disciples were not satisfied with the possessions and positions the Lord had provided them. We see their lack of humility in a conversation that took place as they traveled through Galilee on their way to Capernaum.

> [30]They left that place and passed through Galilee. Jesus did not want anyone to know where they were, [31]because he was teaching his disciples. He said to them, "The Son of Man is going to be delivered into the hands of men. They will kill him, and after three days he will rise." [32]But they did not understand what he meant and were afraid to ask him about it.
>
> [33]They came to Capernaum. When he was in the house, he asked them, "What were you arguing about on the road?" [34]But they kept quiet because on the way they had argued about who was the greatest.
>
> [35]Sitting down, Jesus called the Twelve and said, "Anyone who wants to be first must be the very last, and the servant of all."
>
> (Mark 9:30-35)

On some level, we all aspire to be great from early in life. Most kids, when asked, have seemingly unattainable goals for their future:

> To play for the NFL.
> To be an astronaut.
> To find the cure for cancer.
> To be a billionaire.

I have never heard a school-aged child cite being an accountant as his or her dream. Jobs such as receptionist, bank teller, sanitation worker, fitness instructor, and phlebotomist—all of which are incredibly important, by the way—rarely get the spotlight in our culture. Typically, they are not considered positions of greatness. Yet all are jobs where service is the major focus.

How revolutionary for Jesus to name "servitude" as the goal of discipleship and greatness as the by-product of humility and selfless service.

There are numerous verses in the Bible that address our call to service of others. A few include:

Each of you should use whatever gift you have received to serve others, as faithful stewards of God's grace in its various forms.

(1 Peter 4:10)

Speak up for those who cannot speak for themselves, for the rights of all who are destitute.

Speak up and judge fairly; defend the rights of the poor and needy.

(Proverbs 31:8-9)

Learn to do right; seek justice. Defend the oppressed. Take up the cause of the fatherless; plead the case of the widow.

(Isaiah 1:17)

How amazing that the greatest human who ever walked the earth modeled to His followers to be the least of all.

How inspiring that you and I, no matter our position, awards, education, experience, aptitude, or bank account can be truly great. How? By being humble like Jesus.

Jesus knew what His followers were talking about when they were discussing who was the greatest. These men had been traveling with Jesus for years and knew Him well. They watched as he avoided political aspirations, titles, and self-promotion, yet they chose to argue about greatness. Let's look at the exchange again:

³³When he was in the house, he asked them, "What were you arguing about on the road?" ³⁴But they kept quiet because on the way they had argued about who was the greatest.

³⁵Sitting down, Jesus called the Twelve and said, "Anyone who wants to be first must be the very last, and the servant of all."

(Mark 9:33-35)

Jesus did not ask what they were arguing about because He did not know. He knew. I am confident He wanted them to have the chance to marinate on the discussion to prepare them for what was coming next. They were no doubt humbled knowing that their discussion paled in comparison with the goodness of Jesus.

The disciples also knew to stay quiet because they knew their discussion would not please Him. They were right. But instead of jumping to correct them, He sat down with them. Do not miss this, friend.

"Sitting down" meant He was eye-level with each of them. He did not stand over them with judgment and disgust. He got on their level. And he appealed to their desire for greatness, turning the definition of greatness on its head. He heard their need for being the first and encouraged them to be the last. He understood their want to be catered to and asked them, instead, to cater to the needs of others.

There are times that I struggle to know exactly what God wants me to do, and then, with a passage like this, He makes it crystal clear. Above all, serve others. Period. Not a whole lot of ambiguity there.

> How amazing that the greatest human who ever walked the earth modeled to His followers to be the least of all.

In which areas of your life do you find it easy to serve?

In which areas do you find it more difficult to serve?

In what area do you find yourself wanting to be "great"?

Leaning into Hope

It gives me hope that even those closest to Jesus struggled with humility. As the person who, as a kid, needed someone to applaud when I cleaned my room, the student who needed good grades to feel successful as an academic, and the employee who needs periodic recognition for good work, I am thankful that even the apostles, those who hung out with Jesus every day, were also broken people. Knowing that makes these men more relatable—and encourages me that Jesus will be patient with me when it comes to my desires to be great, but also love me enough to remind me that greatness in the eyes of God is more important than in the eyes of men.

Rather than accuse or rebuke the disciples for arguing about greatness, Jesus asked a question so that they could realize just how foolish their cool contest really was. Questions can serve as colanders, filtering out the waters of foolishness we sometimes sit in and allow us to get to the heart of what matters.

These men were having a contest of sorts—the "greatest debate." Although our contests may not be as obvious, I think each of us faces these types of "contests" in our everyday life:

- social media posts that can make us feel like inferior parents;
- celebrity magazine covers that can make us feel like we don't measure up;
- pictures of friends having fun with others that can make us feel uninvited;
- the academic achievements of others that can make us feel that we do not stack up;
- the confidence of others that can make us feel small;
- the big houses, expensive cars, and extravagant vacations of others that can make us feel lacking, or
- when our spouse pays more attention to work that can make us feel unloved or unseen.

These are less obvious, but equally dangerous contests.

Jesus asked his disciples to take their eyes from themselves and focus on Kingdom work—to serve and love others with humility.

He asks us to do the same thing. Can you imagine what would happen if all who called themselves Christians would lay aside the contests of this world, humble themselves, and focus solely on serving others for His glory? There would not be enough pews in churches, enough services to attend, or enough songs to sing. We would be the sermon—the Word made flesh, the truth of God put into action. Then we would live up to our title: "little Christs" or Christians.

What are some of the awards you have earned in your lifetime? Of which are you most proud?

In your own words, define "greatness" and "humility" in view of Jesus's question to the disciples.

Greatness:

Humility:

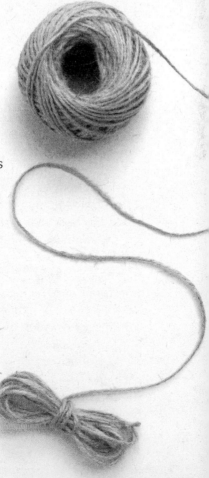

A Practical Next Step

Read Philippians 2:1-11 and list the ways that Jesus showed greatness through humility. Prayerfully meditate on the verses, asking Jesus to show you how these verses connect to your current life experience. How is God inviting you to respond? Write your response to God below:

Day 4 | Following God Means Being Born of the Spirit

Big Idea

We find new life in Jesus by being spiritually reborn.

Jesus's Question:
"If I have told you about earthly things and you don't believe, how will you believe if I tell you about heavenly things?"
(John 3:12 CEB)

The Question We Ask:
How can I have eternal life?

Leaning into the Question

I love sci-fi. I know I lost about 80 percent of you by saying so, but there is something beautiful, scary, and pioneering about a movie set in or about space. They often feel like old Westerns in innovative outfits and complicated sets. The suspension of disbelief for me is actually a very fun adventure. I love the feeling of being "transported" (all puns intended) into space through movies, television shows, and even the occasional soundtrack.

I came by this honestly. My parents, who did not seem to agree on much, especially as I got older, could agree on the appeal of *Star Trek*. Spock, McCoy, Bones, Uhura, Scotty, Chekov, and Sulu were regulars on their television each week and became trusted friends. My parents even loved the hundreds of actors and actresses whose characters died in the episodes, often called the expendable red-shirt crewmen in the original series.

They all were distinct characters, but Captain William T. Kirk (the *T* stands for Tiberius; he was named after his grandfather—and yes, I am a full-fledged nerd) was the captain of the *USS Enterprise* and the largest personality. He was bold, headstrong, charismatic, and honest, having a strong sense of right and wrong even when others did not agree with him. He was charming and would woo every female being on the show—well, almost—but then was brave enough to save an alien people group under attack. Captain Kirk was stubborn; if he felt strongly about something, he would disobey direct orders and take matters into his own hands, much to the chagrin of his crew and delight of his viewers, all while using a clipped, dramatic way of communicating.

But all of that is fake. Captain Kirk is a fictional character (I weep as I type this). There is no real ship, crew, Tribbles, or Starship Federation.

The actor who played Kirk, however, is real. William Shatner has been featured in numerous movies and television shows in his seventy years of acting, has been the inspiration for many *SNL* skits, has been featured in numerous memes, and recently, at the ripe age of ninety, has brushed the edges of earth's atmosphere as a real astronaut for a ten-minute ride he will not soon forget. He accepted an invitation from billionaire Jeff Bezos's company, Blue Origin, to hurl into space in a rocket, a suborbital space tourism rocket funded by the Amazon billionaire. Although he took numerous trips on the *USS Enterprise*, this was the first time the actor had actually been in space.

This nonagenarian found the experience to be truly profound but bittersweet. The usually sanguine and outgoing Shatner displayed emotion and newfound conviction about the environment, saying, "I wish I had better news, and more entertainment, and jokes, to tell you. But I was moved to tears by what I saw. And I come back filled with— overwhelmed by sadness and empathy for this beautiful thing we call Earth."[3]

It wasn't his decades of embodying a space explorer on television that put a fire in his belly for the preservation of the environment; it was a day of actually exploring space.

"What is tragic is if our children . . . , especially our children's children, don't have a chance to be part of this beautiful thing we call Earth. And it's just sad,"[4] Shatner commented. His experience in space seems to have given him a greater perspective on Earth.

Not everyone can afford the trip into space—most flights start at $250,000 and "skyrocket" (pun intended) to $50 million per seat if one leaves the orbit of Earth.[5] But all of us can benefit from a fresh perspective once in a while, including a religious leader who secretly met with Jesus.

Leaning into the Scripture

In the Gospel of John, we encounter this religious leader who had gone through rigorous training, years of memorizing Scripture, and seasons of teaching others the Law of Moses. But when he encountered Jesus, he was given a new perspective that changed everything for him. His name was Nicodemus.

Nicodemus was a member of the Jewish ruling council and a teacher of the Law. Similar to William Shatner's experience, he was about to be given the opportunity to see things from a brand-new perspective. But unlike Shatner's gravity-defying experience, his opportunity to meet with Jesus had eternal gravity (pun intended).

²He came to Jesus at night and said, "Rabbi, we know that you are a teacher who has come from God. For no one could perform the signs you are doing if God were not with him."

³Jesus replied, "Very truly I tell you, no one can see the kingdom of God unless they are born again."

⁴"How can someone be born when they are old?" Nicodemus asked. "Surely they cannot enter a second time into their mother's womb to be born!"

⁵Jesus answered, "Very truly I tell you, no one can enter the kingdom of God unless they are born of water and the Spirit. ⁶Flesh gives birth to flesh, but the Spirit gives birth to spirit. ⁷You should not be surprised at my saying, 'You must be born again.' ⁸The wind blows wherever it pleases. You hear its sound, but you cannot tell where it comes from or where it is going. So it is with everyone born of the Spirit."

⁹"How can this be?" Nicodemus asked.

¹⁰"You are Israel's teacher," said Jesus, "and do you not understand these things? ¹¹Very truly I tell you, we speak of what we know, and we testify to what we have seen, but still you people do not accept our testimony. ¹²I have spoken to you of earthly things and you do not believe; how then will you believe if I speak of heavenly things? ¹³No one has ever gone into heaven except the one who came from heaven—the Son of Man. ¹⁴Just as Moses lifted up the snake in the wilderness, so the Son of Man must be lifted up, ¹⁵that everyone who believes may have eternal life in him."

(John 3:2-15)

Nicodemus represented some of the best and the worst that humanity has to offer. At our best, when we learn the Word of God, we put it into practice and make the world a better place by connecting people to God. But Nicodemus was a religious leader, a member of the Pharisees. Religion, albeit based on good intentions, sometimes can serve to separate people from God through overwhelming rules, abuse, and unattainable rigors—which certainly was true in Jesus's day.

Nicodemus also was curious—arguably a wonderful characteristic of humans—and desired to have Jesus answer some spiritual questions he had. In all his years as a religious scholar, he had never seen someone do such amazing feats as Jesus, and it had made him hungry to learn more about the man behind the miracles.

Nicodemus had a hard time understanding what Jesus was trying to communicate because of his position, his past, and his perspective. As a teacher of the Law and an upholder of religious traditions, he stood to lose everything if the Messiah had come. Jesus gently guided Nicodemus, unpacking spiritual concepts to help him see the truth.

There are a few notable insights from this passage I'd like us to unpack together.

> He came to Jesus **at night** and said, "Rabbi, **we know** that you are a teacher who has come from God. For no one could perform the signs you are doing if God were not with him." *(v. 2, emphasis added)*

Nicodemus likely came at night because he did not want to lose face with the other Pharisees if Jesus proved to be a false prophet. However, because he used the words "we know," it's possible there were other Pharisees who also were curious but not bold enough to make the trek to Jesus.

Nicodemus called Jesus "Rabbi," meaning teacher, even though he was an authority on the Scriptures and a teacher himself. This shows great curiosity and humility—two things most Pharisees were not known for at the time.

> Jesus replied, "Very truly I tell you, no one can see the kingdom of God unless they are born again."

> "**How** can someone be born when they are old?" Nicodemus asked. "Surely they cannot enter a second time into their mother's womb to be born!" *(vv. 3-4, emphasis added)*

Nicodemus's question tells us that he was looking at the things Jesus was saying with human eyes. The same eyes that read, memorized, and taught the teachings of God were missing the Word made flesh—Jesus—and the things He was trying to communicate.

Now, as we've said, Nicodemus was a Pharisee, not one of the Sadducees who did not believe in an afterlife. The Pharisees strictly adhered to the Jewish Scriptures and traditions and were known for their attitude of superiority, but they believed in life after death. So when Nicodemus came to talk to Jesus, he exercised humility and curiosity by asking about spiritual rebirth and concepts of deeper spirituality. Jesus not only gave him spiritual answers; He provided Nicodemus spiritual questions as well. Let's look again at verses 10-15:

> [10]"You are Israel's teacher," said Jesus, "**and do you not understand these things?** [11]Very truly I tell you, we speak of what we know, and we testify to what we have seen, but still you people do not accept our testimony. [12]I have spoken to you of earthly things and you do not believe; **how then will you believe if I speak of heavenly things?** [13]No one has ever gone into

heaven except the one who came from heaven—the Son of Man. [14]*Just as Moses lifted up the snake in the wilderness,* so the Son of Man must be lifted up, [15]that everyone who believes may have eternal life in him."

(John 3:10-15, emphasis added)

After asking Nicodemus about his lack of understanding, Jesus referred to a story Nicodemus would be very familiar with—the snake in the wilderness, from the Book of Numbers—to help Nicodemus comprehend what He was saying.

> [4]*They traveled from Mount Hor along the route to the Red Sea, to go around Edom. But the people grew impatient on the way;* [5]*they spoke against God and against Moses, and said, "Why have you brought us up out of Egypt to die in the wilderness? There is no bread! There is no water! And we detest this miserable food!"*
>
> [6]*Then the Lord sent venomous snakes among them; they bit the people and many Israelites died.* [7]*The people came to Moses and said, "We sinned when we spoke against the Lord and against you. Pray that the Lord will take the snakes away from us." So Moses prayed for the people.*
>
> [8]*The Lord said to Moses, "Make a snake and put it up on a pole; anyone who is bitten can look at it and live."* [9]**So Moses made a bronze snake and put it up on a pole. Then when anyone was bitten by a snake and looked at the bronze snake, they lived.**

(Numbers 21:4-9, emphasis added)

Just as God provided a way to take the Israelites from death to life through Moses lifting up the snake, so God sent Jesus to take believers from death to life through His sacrifice on the cross:

> For God so loved the world that he gave his one and only Son, that whoever believes in him shall not perish but have eternal life.

(John 3:16)

Long before John 3:16 was a sign at a football game, a bumper sticker on a car, a theme for VBS, or a tattoo, it was a message from Jesus to Nicodemus—and to the whole world.

Jesus offered life eternal, the greatest hope of all, to this religious man who had questions—and He offers it to you and me.

Through Jesus's encounter with Nicodemus, we have insights and hope pointing us to eternal life in Him. Jesus confirms through His conversation with Nicodemus that those dead in their sins can find new life in Him by being spiritually reborn,

God sent Jesus to take believers from death to life through His sacrifice on the cross.

and those dead in the body can have spiritual life after death through faith in Him. When we put our faith in Jesus, death leads to life!

Reread John 3:1-16 in your Bible. What does it mean to be born again? According to Jesus, how do we have eternal life?

When did you first accept Jesus as your personal Lord and Savior? What helped you to understand and believe? If you have not yet made this decision, what questions stand in your way?

Leaning into Hope

Though we cannot relate to being a religious leader in the time of Jesus, we all can relate to having questions!

Nicodemus had a hard time understanding Jesus because of his position, his past, and his perspective as a religious leader. We too come face to face with our own position, past, and perspective when choosing whether or not to accept Jesus as our personal Lord and Savior:

- First, we have to give up our position as the boss of our lives (Romans 10:9-10 and Romans 12:1).
- Then, when we repent of our sins and accept the forgiveness of God through Jesus, we must sacrifice the things of the past by becoming a new creation in Christ (2 Corinthians 5:17).
- And when we become a believer, God calls us to a new perspective—a life where we deny ourselves, take up our cross daily, and follow Him (Luke 9:23).

Those of us who are in Christ—who not only believe but also have given our lives to Him—are given amazing gifts: the forgiveness of our sins, the hope of eternal life, the love of the Father, the sacrifice of the Son for us, and the indwelling of the Holy Spirit. When we understand the gravity of these gifts, our first response is gratitude, and then we respond to the gifts by "applying them" in our daily lives—by living differently. What does this look like?

Let's look again at some of the most encouraging words in Scripture found in the story of Nicodemus:

For God so loved the world that he gave his one and only Son, that whoever believes in him shall not perish but have eternal life.

(John 3:16)

If we look closely, we see there are five verbs included in this verse:
1. loved,
2. gave,
3. believe,
4. not perish, and
5. have (eternal life).

As those who follow Jesus, we want to put these verbs into practice as we walk with Him and grow in our faith, encouraging one another along with way. Specifically, we want to

1. love God, others, and ourselves;
2. give generously through our words, actions, attitudes, and finances;
3. bolster our belief through prayer and study of God's Word;
4. nurture life and growth by speaking life and doing activities that give life to us and to others; and
5. live with a Kingdom perspective as those who have the joy and hope of life eternal.

This is how we live when we are born of the Spirit. This is what it means to follow God. Rather than a spiritual checklist, these actions become our desires when we draw close to Jesus and say yes to Him. Rather than a one-time response that brings instantaneous transformation, we respond continually in an ongoing process of growth, just as a baby becomes a child and then an adolescent and then an adult. Spiritual rebirth is the beginning of a never-ending journey of joy and hope in our Savior. And Jesus promises to be by our side every step of the way.

If you are a believer, how has following Jesus given you new life and hope? If you have not yet made this decision, what questions do you have about following Jesus, and who might be someone you could talk to about them?

In which of the five ways above do you need to put your faith into practice? What are some other ways you follow Jesus each day?

What are you most excited about when it comes to following Jesus?

A Practical Next Step

If you, like Nicodemus, have questions about believing in God, being reborn spiritually, and having eternal life, ask questions! Find someone you trust to discuss these questions with. Search the Scriptures that talk about placing your faith in Jesus, eternal life, and heaven. Here are a few to get you started:

Old Testament	New Testament
Jeremiah 32:17	Matthew 6:19-20; 19:14, 21; 24:35
Psalm 19:1-2	Luke 24:50-51
Psalm 73:24-25	John 3:16; 6:40, 47; 10:28-30; 14:1-2, 6; 17:3
Psalm 108:5	Acts 1:9; 4:12
Psalm 124:8	Romans 6:22-23; 10:9-10, 17
Proverbs 8:35	2 Corinthians 5:1, 21
Isaiah 25:6-9; 26:19	Ephesians 2:8-9
Jeremiah 23:24	Philippians 3:20
Ezekiel 18:32	Colossians 3:2
Amos 9:6	1 Thessalonians 4:16-17
	1 Timothy 6:7-8
	2 Timothy 4:7-8, 18
	1 John 3:2-3; 5:11-13
	Revelation 21:3-4

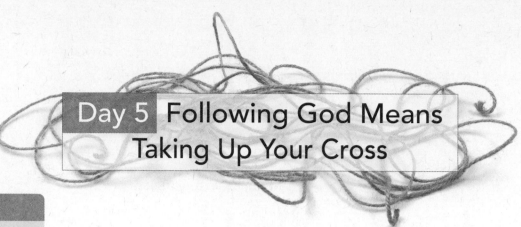

Day 5 Following God Means Taking Up Your Cross

Big Idea

The rewards of following Jesus far outweigh the costs.

Jesus's Question:
*What good will it be for someone to gain the whole world,
yet forfeit their soul?*
(Matthew 16:26)

The Question We Ask:
What do I have to give up for Jesus?

Leaning into the Question

When my husband and I were first married, we were what some call "poor as church mice." I think it was more like church beetles, but that is another story.

We shared an old car, rarely went out to eat, and lived in an old apartment building filled with university students, cockroaches, and other poor newlyweds—but it got the job done.

The bathroom was so small that one could not sit on the toilet and open the door simultaneously. Once when I fainted due to an adverse reaction to a new medication, it took my poor husband almost ten minutes to pry my unconscious body out of the bathroom. When I awoke, my leg hurt because my husband had to forcefully press the door against it numerous times. That bruise lasted for weeks!

One day I was sitting in that same palatial powder room doing the business one does in such a room when it started. Like a scene from *Willie Wonka and the Chocolate Factory*, brown liquid began to seep from the ceiling of the bathroom, including the space above my head. As quickly as I could, I hopped up from the seat, pulled up the clothes from around my ankles, and ran out of the bathroom, yelling, "There's stuff coming from the ceiling! It's brown!"

We didn't know the official "brown liquid coming from the ceiling" protocol, so I called the apartment management company as my husband ran upstairs to the apartment above. The walls were so thin, I could clearly hear my husband pounding on the door of the apartment. After a few rounds of knocking, I heard the door open and muffled voices exchanging words.

Then the brown liquid stopped dripping.

It seems that the man who lived above us had needed to de-stress, had started a bath, and then had fallen asleep. The bathtub began to overflow, seeping through his floor to our ceiling (thus the brown color). When all was said and done, the tenant had to pay nearly $12,000 for the repairs. His search for relaxation took an expensive and unforeseen turn, leading to more stress.

We all learned a lot that day.

My husband learned that in an emergency, he really can run fast.

Our upstairs neighbor learned that setting a timer might be a good idea when drawing a bath.

And I learned that even clear water, when it goes through the filter of the building materials of an old apartment building, looks different on the other side.

We all have had experiences that teach us something about ourselves, make us wiser, and change our perspective.

In Matthew 16, Jesus attempts to explain that the cost of following Him involves all three.

Leaning into the Scripture

Disciple is a word that means "a person who is a pupil or an adherent of the doctrines of another; follower."[6] In Matthew 16, Jesus begins to explain to his inner circle about the rights, responsibilities, and privileges of being a disciple and following Him. He is imparting a kind of mission statement or job description to his twelve disciples:

> [24]*Then Jesus said to his disciples, "Whoever wants to be my disciple must deny themselves and take up their cross and follow me.* [25]*For whoever wants to save their life will lose it, but whoever loses their life for me will find it.* [26]**What good will it be for someone to gain the whole world, yet forfeit their soul?** *Or what can anyone give in exchange for their soul?* [27]*For the Son of Man is going to come in his Father's glory with his angels, and then he will reward each person according to what they have done."*
>
> (Matthew 16:24-27, emphasis added)

Jesus warns his disciples—and us—in these verses not to pursue the things of this world with such fervor that they lose fervor for the things of heaven.

The lesson Jesus is articulating here is that the world's priorities are not God's priorities. The world prioritizes possessions, power, and position, whereas God prioritizes poverty of spirit and humility and servanthood. In addition, Jesus makes it clear what He is asking us to give up, our own plans and agenda for our lives, and what He promises us in return, not just rewards in heaven but eternal, abundant life that begins here and now and continues forever.

When we give up the false self, our fleshly desires, and are willing to sacrifice and serve, we actually find abundant life in becoming our most authentic selves. We don't lose who we are but, instead, become who God made us to be.

How do you find yourself pursuing the world's priorities of possessions, power, and position—sometimes without intention or awareness?

> We find abundant life in becoming our most authentic selves.

What are some specific ways you are pursuing or would like to pursue God's priorities of poverty of spirit, humility, and servanthood?

What does "losing your life" as expressed in this verse mean to you?

What would it mean to you to experience abundant life and find your authentic self?

Leaning into Hope

When first glancing at the cost of following Jesus, it can seem daunting indeed, but only if we focus on the cost alone. Considering what we *gain* changes our perspective.

There is an amazing Cirque du Soleil show called *LOVE* that is an amazing reimagining of Beatles music through circus-style performance currently playing at the Mirage Theatre in Las Vegas.

Years ago, my husband surprised me with tickets to see this spectacle. He got a sitter for our kids, removed work stressors, gassed up the vehicle, got spiffed up for the evening, and drove us from our home in Arizona to the theater in Las Vegas (about a four-hour drive)—all so I could enjoy the evening.

I am a huge Beatles fan. I know every word to every song. So, this show was a dream come true.

We arrived early (we do not like to miss anything) and found our seats. I asked him if I could see the ticket because often Cirque du Soleil show tickets are full of artistry and creativity as well. As he handed me the ticket and I held it in my hand, I nearly threw up.

When I saw the cost of the ticket, I began to do the math in my head for how much this ninety-minute show was costing us per minute—times two plus gas, hotel room (it would be a late evening), babysitter, and food.

My sweet husband watched all the blood drain from my face. When I explained what I was thinking, no amount of convincing on his part was working to soothe my brain or heart. In that moment I felt that the cost was ridiculous, outlandish, unreasonable, unfair, and irresponsible.

Before the show started, I was determined not to like it. But with each passing minute after the curtain opened, I went from public accountant in my head to child in my heart. The performances were electrifying, the sets were magical, the music was invigorating, and the storytelling was inspired.

All thoughts of the cost dissipated, and at the end of the show, I turned to my husband and said, "We have got to bring the kids to see this!" The cost of the show quickly became inconsequential when compared to the benefits I experienced, and I could not wait for my favorite people to experience it themselves.

A similar thing is true of discipleship. Read Matthew 16:24-27 again, and then list the costs and rewards of following Jesus in the chart below.

Then Jesus said to his disciples, "Whoever wants to be my disciple must deny themselves and take up their cross and follow me. For whoever wants to save their life will lose it, but whoever loses their life for me will find it. What good will it be for someone to gain the whole world, yet forfeit their soul? Or what can anyone give in exchange for their soul? For the Son of Man is going to come in his Father's glory with his angels, and then he will reward each person according to what they have done."

(Matthew 16:24-27)

Costs	Rewards

The promises that Jesus makes to those who follow Him include life abundant here on earth and life eternal with Him after we die. These rewards are far greater than any show could depict, actor could portray, or ticket could buy.

We can find great comfort and hope in knowing that Jesus not only encourages us to follow Him but also promises to be with us always—here on earth and all the way to heaven, where He will reward us for our pursuit. Regardless of what any of us might have to give up to follow Jesus, we can be certain that the rewards of following Him far outweigh the costs!

For you, what is the most daunting cost of following Jesus, and why?

For you, what is the greatest reward of following Jesus, and why?

> We can find great comfort and hope in knowing that Jesus not only encourages us to follow Him but also promises to be with us always.

A Practical Next Step

Ask God to help you write a personal mission statement for following Jesus, referring to the description of discipleship that Jesus gives us in Matthew 16:24-27. Allow this to be a prayerful process. You might even want to reflect and work on it over a period of days or weeks. When you're ready, share it with someone you trust.

Week 6 | Wrap-up

It was a funeral service I will not soon forget.

Although I did not know the departed well, I had recently befriended his bride. Out of respect and care for her, when her husband, Ron, fell ill, my husband and I had taken them dinner and spent a lovely evening with the two of them.

Weeks later, Ron was gone.

At the funeral, the sanctuary seats were filled with friends, family, community leaders, church folks, and coworkers. The message was well delivered and the music was delightful, but one of the stories shared by a friend made a lasting impression on me.

The friend explained that for many years he and Ron had been in Bible study together, had attended the same church, had done life together, and had shared many glasses of wine. Now, I understand that wine can be a sensitive topic for a

variety of reasons, including addiction concerns. But regardless of what you think about drinking, I hope you'll stick with me and see why I chose to include this story—because I believe it points us to a powerful message.

The friend continued, saying that when Ron had major heart surgery, he went to the hospital to pray with Ron and his wife before the surgery. Ron promised him that if he survived the surgery, the two of them would drink some of the wine on the right side of the wine fridge—the location of some very exclusive and expensive bottles of wine that Ron had been collecting over the years.

Well, Ron survived alright, and so, as promised, the men dove into the exclusive wine collection only to find that much of it had gone bad. Any wine drinker knows that storage problems, poor bottling techniques, oxidation, and even microbial contamination can turn even the finest vino into undrinkable swill. Thousands of dollars' worth of vintage grapes were poured down the drain that night.

The friend encouraged all in attendance to avoid having a "right side of the fridge" mentality—the idea of saving the best for "someday." In other words, we should live each day of life fully—in all of our relationships, actions, and decisions. It was a great story giving insight into how we should live—as if each day is our last. That's not the powerful message I mentioned, but it points us to it. You see, truly abundant and full life is possible only because of Jesus. Jesus came and died and rose again so that we might have life to the full—eternal life that starts now, not someday in the future.

One of the ways I have found to live life fully is to examine the things Jesus said and did—the way He served, the lives He touched, the love He showed, and the questions He asked.

When Jesus posed over three hundred questions in the Bible, He also gave us insight into how to follow Him. This week we have examined some of those insights, such as offering compassion instead of judgment, practicing empathy, being humble, being born of the Spirit, and taking up your cross.

He also gave us the gift of questions. In a day when we have the answers to millions of questions at our fingertips via the internet on our phones, some people find unanswered questions uncomfortable. But if we are willing to sit in the discomfort of our questions and continue to seek the face and truth of God, the payoff can have eternal ramifications—a deeper, richer relationship with God that begins now and continues for all eternity!

Of the questions we've explored, which one resonates most, and why?

What questions do you still have related to following Christ?

Read the week's memory verse, Micah 6:8, slowly several times. Is there a word or phrase that catches your attention or touches your heart? What does God have to say to you about the word or phrase in light of your current life experience? How is God inviting you to respond?

Video Viewer Guide Week 6

What Does It Mean to Follow God?

Memory Verse:

Micah 6:8 NIV

Past:

He has shown you...what is _____.

Position:

He has shown you, O _____

Pondering:

And what does the Lord _____ _____ _____?

_____ To act justly

_____ To love mercy

_____ To walk humbly with your God.

Permission Slip:

This week, we unpacked what it means to be a follower and disciple of Jesus. Although He has a plan for each of us that includes a hope and a future, His plan also includes our redeemed past, and a present that is rooted in Him.

You have permission to _____ _____ _____.

Final Thoughts on *Untangling Faith*

Oftentimes we approach a study looking for answers. My prayer for you at the end of this study about questions is that you have more curiosity, more wonder, and more freedom to continue to be openhanded and openhearted in your pursuit of the Lord.

Keep Asking

Every time we ask a question, it can lead us on our journey to a deeper and fuller understanding of God. Some people, when exploring faith, are afraid of uncertainty; but as we've seen, Jesus welcomes our questions while encouraging us to believe. When He addressed uncertainty, He affirmed those who believe without the certainty of sight:

> Then Jesus told him, "Because you have seen me, you have believed; blessed are those who have not seen and yet have believed."

(John 20:29)

Keep Following

When God appeared to His people in the wilderness, He appeared not as a translucent cloud, difficult to identify, but as a dense cloud, easy to see. In Exodus 13:21-22, God promises to lead the Israelites by a pillar of cloud by day and a pillar of fire at night. Then in Exodus 19:9, God explains that he will speak to Moses in the dense cloud. A dense cloud is the perfect choice to communicate that God is present yet undefinable, relational yet incomprehensible, knowable yet mysterious, and familiar yet miraculous.

From the beginning of their Exodus from Egypt, God led them on their journey to a new land and a new and deeper understanding of Him.

In the New Testament, Jesus led His followers similarly. Although He was present in flesh and bone that they could see and touch, Jesus invited the disciples to "Come, follow me" (Mark 1:17). They didn't know Him or know how to follow Him until they answered the call and began following. We learn about Jesus "on the way."

Keep Trusting

When the Old Testament prophet Jeremiah had questions about his situation, he was encouraged by God to trust Him with his questions:

> *"Call to me and I will answer you and tell you great and unsearchable things you do not know."*
>
> (Jeremiah 33:3)

We can trust God with our questions too, confident that God will answer us.

Keep Untangling

Ultimately, Jesus tells us what the Greatest Commandment is:

> *"Love the Lord your God with all your heart and with all your soul and with all your mind."*
>
> (Matthew 22:37)

God is after our whole being. Asking questions broadens not only our head knowledge of God but also our heart-and-soul knowledge of God—our understanding and experience of God's goodness and love in every circumstance, which bolsters our faith, encourages our hearts, and enriches our souls. As a popular adaptation of the old proverb goes, "curiosity may kill the cat, but it fuels the lion." In other words, curiosity helps us to become brave and strong as we ask, seek, and knock just as Jesus instructed us to do (Matthew 7:7).

If we are going to untangle our faith and grow spiritually, the questions of Jesus are a great place to start, providing a lens through which we can explore our own questions. Let us continue to be people of faith who bring our curiosity to God without fear, trusting the God who gave us the capacity to ask questions in the first place and who loves us beyond comprehension.

God's richest blessings on your journey!

> *"The Lord bless you and keep you; the Lord make his face shine on you and be gracious to you; the Lord turn his face toward you and give you peace."*
>
> (Numbers 6:24-26)

Amberly

> Curiosity helps us to become brave and strong as we ask, seek, and knock just as Jesus instructed us to do.

Video Viewer Guide Answers

Week 1

strength

shield

helps

trusts

joy

praise

doubts

Week 2

tell

mustard seed

will move

Nothing

get it right

Week 3

confidence / approaching

his will

hears

wonder

Week 4

Praise

Worship

forget not

forgives

heals

redeems

crowns

ask

Week 5

Show

Guide / teach

hope

uncertain

Week 6

good

mortal

require of you

Act

Adore

Accompany

need reminders

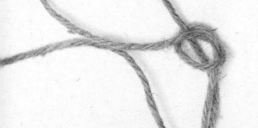

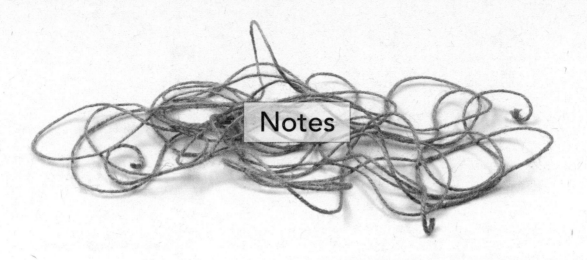

Notes

Week 1: Can I Trust God?

1. *Merriam-Webster*, s.v. "trust," accessed November 1, 2022, https://www.merriam-webster.com/dictionary/trust.
2. *Barnes' Notes*, s.v. "Matthew 16:6," https://biblehub.com/commentaries/barnes/matthew/16.htm.
3. Ellen Gutoskey, "When the Star of Titanic Helped Pay the Bills for the Last Titanic Survivor," September 24, 2021, https://www.mentalfloss.com/article/650575/when-titanic-stars-donated-money-last-titanic-survivor?utm_medium=email&utm_source=Daily_Newsletter; and Biography, s.v. "Millvina Dean," April 2, 2014, https://www.biography.com/historical-figure/millvina-dean.

Week 2: How Can I Grow in My Faith?

1. Jessica Leigh Hester, "Way Before Roller Coasters, Russians Zipped Down Enormous Ice Slides," Atlas Obscura, August 21, 2019, https://www.atlasobscura.com/articles/russian-roller-coasters.
2. Michele Debczak, "The Teddy Roosevelt–Inspired Roller Coaster that Killed 7 People at Coney Island," Mental Floss, July 14, 2020, https://www.mentalfloss.com/article/626458/coney-island-deadly-rough-rider-roller-coaster.
3. Peter Ward, "Coney Island's Roller Coaster History," Culture Trip, June 16, 2017, https://theculturetrip.com/north-america/usa/new-york/articles/coney-islands-roller-coaster-history/.
4. Nashia Baker, "The Chinese Artifact Purchased for $35 at a Connecticut Yard Sale Just Sold for $722,000," Martha Stewart, March 18, 2021, https://www.marthastewart.com/8077388/connecticut-yard-sale-bowl-chinese-artifact-auctioned.

Week 3: Why Should I Pray?

1. "Our History—The U-Haul Story," https://www.uhaul.com/About/History/, accessed November 1, 2022.
2. Franz Lidz, "She Fell Nearly 2 Miles, and Walked Away," *New York Times*, https://www.nytimes.com/2021/06/18/science/koepcke-diller-panguana-amazon-crash.html, June 18, 2021; updated October 3, 2021.
3. "Matthew Henry's Commentary on James 5:16-18," Christianity.com, https://www.christianity.com/bible/niv/james/5-16-18.
4. David Guzik, "Luke 13—Repentance, False Religion and the True Way," Enduring Word, 2018, https://enduringword.com/bible-commentary/luke-13/.
5. Guzik, "Luke 13."

Week 4: What Must I Do to Be Healed?

1. Reuters Staff, "British Vicar Catches Fire Waiting for God's Answer," March 24, 2020, https://www.reuters.com/article/us-health-coronavirus-britain-vicar/british-vicar-catches-fire-waiting-for-gods-answer-idUSKBN21C0GM.
2. Reuters Staff, "British Vicar Catches Fire Waiting for God's Answer."
3. *The KJV New Testament Greek Lexicon*, s.v. "Soteria," https://www.biblestudytools.com/lexicons/greek/kjv/soteria.html.

Week 5: What Is God's Plan for Us?

1. *Strong's Concordance*, s.v. "zakar," December 5, 2022, https://biblehub.com/hebrew/2142.htm.
2. *Merriam-Webster*, s.v. "season," December 5, 2022, https://www.merriam-webster.com/dictionary/season.
3. Encyclopedia.com, s.v. "Sadducees," December 5, 2022, https://www.encyclopedia.com/philosophy-and-religion/judaism/judaism/sadducees.
4. Meg Bucher, "8 Things to Know About the Sadducees in the Bible," December 16, 2021, https://www.crosswalk.com/faith/bible-study/things-to-know-about-the-sadducees-in-the-bible.html.
5. Bucher, "8 Things to Know About the Sadducees in the Bible."
6. Dictionary.com, s.v. "entertain," December 5, 2022, https://www.dictionary.com/browse/entertain.

Week 6: What Does It Mean to Follow God?

1. Dan Brekke, "Boomtown Memories: The Nob Hill Fence That Spite Built," KQED, March 6, 2015, https://www.kqed.org/news/10449405/boomtown-memories-the-nob-hill-fence-that-spite-built.
2. Jake Rossen, "The Man Who Built a 40-Foot Spite Fence Around His Neighbor's Home," April 24, 2017, Mental Floss, https://www.mentalfloss.com/article/94298/crocker-spite-fence-san-francisco.
3. William Shatner, interview by Chris Cuomo, *Cuomo Prime Time*, CNN, October 14, 2021, https://transcripts.cnn.com/show/CPT/date/2021-10-14/segment/01.
4. Shatner, interview by Chris Cuomo.
5. Bruno Venditti, "The Cost of Space Flight Before and After SpaceX," Visual Capitalist, January 27, 2022, https://www.visualcapitalist.com/the-cost-of-space-flight/#:~:text=Space%20Tourism&text=For%20a%20suborbital%20trip%20on,than%20%2450%20million%20per%20seat.
6. Dictionary.com, s.v. "disciple," December 8, 2022, https://www.dictionary.com/browse/disciple.

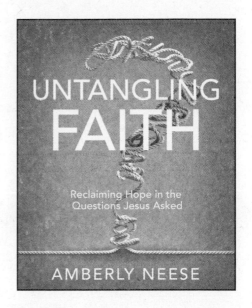